CONTENTS

PART ONE
INTRODUCTION

PART TWO
SUMMARIES

PART THREE
COMMENTARY

PART FOUR
RESOURCES

PREFACE

York Notes are designed to give you a broader perspective on works of literature studied at GCSE and equivalent levels. With examination requirements changing in the twenty-first century, we have made a number of significant changes to this new series. We continue to help students to reach their own interpretations of the text but York Notes now have important extra-value new features.

You will discover that York Notes are genuinely interactive. The new **Checkpoint** features make sure that you can test your knowledge and broaden your understanding. You will also be directed to excellent websites, books and films where you can follow up ideas for yourself.

The **Resources** section has been updated and an entirely new section has been devoted to how to improve your grade. Careful reading and application of the principles laid out in the Resources section guarantee improved performance.

The **Detailed summaries** include an easy-to-follow skeleton structure of the poems, while the section on **Language and style** has been extended to offer an in-depth discussion of the poets' techniques.

The Contents page shows the structure of this study guide. However, there is no need to read from the beginning to the end as you would with a novel, play or poem. Use the Notes in the way that suits you. Our aim is to help you with your understanding of the poem, not to dictate how you should learn.

Our authors are practising English teachers and examiners who have used their experience to offer a whole range of **Examiner's secrets** – useful hints to encourage exam success.

The General Editor of this series is John Polley, Senior GCSE Examiner and former Head of English at Harrow Way Community School, Andover.

The author of these Notes is Geoff Brookes who is Deputy Headteacher of Cefn Hengoed Comprehensive School in Swansea and has been an English teacher and examiner at all levels for 30 years, initially at Gateway Sixth Form College in Leicester. He is also a freelance writer and his work has appeared in a variety of publications.

The text used in these Notes is the AQA Anthology for GCSE English/English Literature (Specification A for 2004).

PART ONE

INTRODUCTION

HOW TO STUDY A POEM

A poem differs from a piece of prose writing because it is freer in its structure, and it often contains a deliberate rhyme and/or rhythm. When reading a poem, each of these aspects should be considered:

STRUCTURE: The poet has made conscious choices to organise the poem as it appears on the page. Try to understand the poet's thinking behind:

- The organisation of the lines (e.g. into verses)

- Any repetition of lines or varying lengths of line

- Whether lines are end-stopped or whether the sense carries over to the next line

RHYME: Consider the rhyming scheme and ask yourself these questions:

- What, if any, is the rhyming scheme?

- Are the rhymes exact or approximate and for what purpose?

- Do some lines have rhyming words within them and why?

- If there are no rhymes, why does the line end where it does?

RHYTHM: Turn to the rhythm of the poem and listen for:

- Which words are stressed

- Whether there is a pattern of sound which creates a mood

- Whether this mood suits the subject matter

SUBJECT MATTER AND THEME: Just like a novel or a play, a poem has a subject matter and a theme. Once you have identified these, consider why the poet has drawn on that particular subject matter to illustrate an idea or develop the theme.

DID YOU KNOW?

The word 'poetry' comes from the Greek word *poesis*, meaning 'making' or 'creating'. People have been writing poetry for thousands of years – the earliest we have dates back to about 3000 BC.

HEANEY/CLARKE – LIFE AND WORKS

1937 Gillian Clarke born in Cardiff

1939 Seamus Heaney born in County Londonderry

1951 Seamus Heaney enters St Columbs

1957 Heaney attends Queen's University, Belfast

1964 Heaney: *Digging* and *Storm on the Island* published

1965 Heaney marries Marie Devlin

1966 Heaney: *Death of a Naturalist*

1972 Clarke: *Snow on the Mountains*. Heaney moves to Irish Republic

1974 Clarke is tutor at College of Art, Newport

1975 Heaney moves to Dublin

1976 Heaney is Head of Caryford Teacher Training College

1978 Clarke: *The Sundial*

1982 Clarke: *Letters from a Far Country*. Heaney becomes poet in residence, Harvard University, Boston, USA

1989 Heaney becomes Professor of Poetry, Oxford University. Clarke: *Letting in the Rumour*

1990 Clarke founds Ty Newydd, the writer's centre in North Wales

CONTEXT

1937 Coronation of George VI

1939 Outbreak of Second World War

1945 End of Second World War

1952 Accession of Queen Elizabeth II

1957 Creation of European Common Market

1964 Nelson Mandela sentenced to life imprisonment in South Africa

1965 Death of Winston Churchill

1966 Aberfan disaster

1972 'Bloody Sunday' shootings in Derry, Northern Ireland

1974 Resignation of President Nixon

1975 Sex Discrimination Act and Equal Pay Act come into force

1976 Death of Chairman Mao

1978 Birth of first 'test-tube' baby

1982 Falklands War

1989 Hillsborough football disaster

1990 Release of Nelson Mandela

1991 Collapse of Yugoslavia

HEANEY/CLARKE – LIFE AND WORKS

1993 Clarke: *King of Britain's Daughter*

1994 Clarke is tutor in Creative Writing, University of Glamorgan

1995 Heaney receives the Noble Prize for Literature

1996 Heaney is awarded the Whitbread Prize for *The Spirit Level*

1997 Clarke: *Trying the Line*

1998 Clarke: *Five Fields*

1999 Heaney is awarded the Whitbread prize for *Beowulf*

CONTEXT

1993 British and Irish Governments sign Northern Ireland Peace Pact

1994 Nelson Mandela becomes President of South Africa

1995 Oklahoma City bombing

1997 Death of Princess Diana

1998 Good Friday Peace Deal

1999 Paddington rail crash

2001 Terrorist attack on New York

PRE-1914 POETS – LIFE AND WORKS

CONTEXT

	1558 Accession of Queen Elizabeth I
1564 William Shakespeare born	**1564** Death of Michelangelo
1572 Ben Jonson born	**1586** Treaty of Berwick establishes a defensive alliance between England and Scotland
1586 Execution of Charles Tichborne. *Tichborne's Elegy* published	
	1587 Execution of Mary, Queen of Scots
1609 Shakespeare's *Sonnets* published	**1588** Defeat of the Spanish Armada
1616 Death of William Shakespeare. *On my first Sonne*, Ben Jonson	**1603** Death of Queen Elizabeth I
	1608 Galileo first uses the telescope
1637 Death of Ben Jonson	**1769** Birth of Napoleon
1730 Oliver Goldsmith born	**1770** Steam engine patented; James Cook discovered New South Wales
1757 William Blake born	
1770 Wordsworth born. *The Village Schoolmaster*, Oliver Goldsmith	**1776** Declaration of American Independence
1774 Death of Oliver Goldsmith	
1789 *The Little Boy Lost*, William Blake. *The Little Boy Found*, William Blake	**1789** French Revolution
	1793 First free English settlers in Australia
1793 John Clare born	**1807** Britain abolishes slave trade
1807 *The Affliction of Margaret*, William Wordsworth	**1809** Charles Darwin born
	1812 First tin cans produced in England for preserving food
1809 Alfred Tennyson born	
1812 Robert Browning born	**1815** Battle of Waterloo
1819 Walt Whitman born	**1819** Peterloo Massacre
1827 Death of William Blake	**1827** First successful photograph taken
1840 Thomas Hardy born	**1837** Accession of Queen Victoria
1841 *Sonnet*, John Clare	**1840** Penny postage stamp introduced
1842 *Ulysses*, Alfred Tennyson	**1842** British massacred in Khyber Pass

PRE-1914 POETS – LIFE AND WORKS	CONTEXT
1844 Gerard Manley Hopkins born	**1844** First Factory Act
1845 *My Last Duchess*, Robert Browning *The Laboratory*, Robert Browning	**1845** Irish Potato Famine
	1848 General revolutionary movement throughout Europe
1850 Death of Wordsworth. Tennyson becomes Poet Laureate	**1850** Creation of jeans by Oscar Levi Strauss for Californian gold prospectors
1851 *The Eagle*, Alfred Tennyson	**1851** The Great Exhibition in London
1856 *Patrolling Barnegat*, Walt Whitman	**1856** End of the Crimean War
	1859 Darwin's *On the Origin of Species*
1864 Death of John Clare	**1861** Outbreak of American Civil War
1865 William B. Yeats born	**1865** End of American Civil War
1881 *Inversnaid*, Gerard Manley Hopkins	**1881** Birth of Pablo Picasso
1884 Tennyson becomes a Baron	**1888** The 'Jack the Ripper' murders
1889 Death of Robert Browning. Death of Gerard Manley Hopkins	**1889** Birth of Adolf Hitler
1892 Death of Alfred, Lord Tennyson. Death of Walt Whitman	
	1899 Outbreak of Boer War
1899 *The Song of the Old Mother*, W. B. Yeats	**1901** Death of Queen Victoria
1902 *The Man He Killed*, Thomas Hardy	**1902** End of Boer War
	1912 Sinking of *Titanic*
	1914 Outbreak of First World War
1918 Hopkins' poetry published	**1918** End of First World War
	1926 Birth of Queen Elizabeth II
1928 Death of Thomas Hardy	**1928** Discovery of penicillin
1937 Birth of Gillian Clarke	**1937** Accession of George VI
1939 Death of William B. Yeats. Birth of Seamus Heaney	**1939** Outbreak of Second World War

CHECK THE BOOK

Seamus Heaney Selected Poems by Shay Daly in the York Notes series is a good introduction to his work.

DID YOU KNOW?

His translation of *Beowulf* won the 1999 Whitbread Book of the Year Award, beating J.K. Rowling's *Harry Potter and the Prisoner of Azkaban* by one vote.

DID YOU KNOW?

Alfred Nobel, the Swedish inventor of dynamite, left $9 million in his will to set up the Nobel Prize Foundation. First presented in 1901, winners receive a diploma, money and a gold medal.

SETTING AND BACKGROUND

SEAMUS HEANEY

Seamus Heaney was born in 1939 in County Londonderry, Northern Ireland. He was the eldest of nine children and his parents lived on a farm called Mossbawn, but any suggestion that he might follow in their footsteps was dismissed because of his academic potential.

He attended St Columb's College in Londonderry (the school referred to in '**Mid-Term Break**') and then went to Queen's University in Belfast where he studied English Language and Literature. It was as an undergraduate that he first started to write and his work appeared in the university magazine.

He initially trained as a teacher at St Joseph's College in Belfast. After a short time as a teacher in St Thomas' Secondary School, he returned to St Joseph's as a lecturer before later returning to Queen's to lecture in English.

In 1965 he married Marie Devlin and together they have three children, Michael, Christopher and Catherine.

His first published collection of poems, *Death of a Naturalist,* was well received. The work in this collection, from which the poems selected here are taken, deal with his childhood and loss of innocence. It won a number of awards and was praised for its vivid depiction of rural life and the landscape of Northern Ireland. Seamus Heaney was described as 'a true poet of considerable importance' (Michael Longley).

In 1970 he spent a year at the University of California, the beginning of a long relationship with America. He has taught for many years at Harvard University.

Volumes of poetry have appeared at regular intervals such as *North* (1975), *Station Island* (1984) and *The Spirit Level* (1996). In these books he has moved from the context of his childhood to deal with wider issues such as the violent politics of Northern Ireland.

Seamus Heaney has worked in a number of academic institutions, establishing his reputation as one of the finest living poets. He has also written plays and translations and books of critical essays. In 1989 he was appointed as Professor of Poetry at Oxford University where he remained until 1994. He is a very learned man yet his work is characterised by its clear and direct style and has brought him acclaim across the world. He is admired by other poets like Ted Hughes as well as by a loyal readership. In 1995 he was awarded the Nobel Prize for Literature in recognition of his achievement. His citation said that his work is notable for its 'lyrical beauty and ethical depth which exalt everyday miracles and the living past'

GILLIAN CLARKE

Gillian Clarke was born in Cardiff, Wales, in 1937 and has lived and worked in Wales for almost all her life. She went to primary school in Barry and then St Clare's Convent school in Porthcawl before taking a degree in English at Cardiff University. She did work for eighteen months as a researcher for the BBC in London, but returned to live in Wales, to marry and to bring up her family – a daughter and two sons. She has also lectured in Art History and in Creative Writing

She began to write and publish poetry in her thirties, encouraged by her first husband. Her work first appeared in a magazine called *Poetry Wales*. Her first collection of poems, *Snow on the Mountains*, was published in 1972. Her first poems established some of the themes that have underpinned most of her work. Her poems are rooted in daily life for she is aware that no lives are untouched by birth and death, love and suffering. She also writes about the role and achievements of women. She says:

> it's good that women poets are speaking up and their work is studied at school. We studied only the dead men at school and university, and wonderful as the dead men are, to read only their work skewed the view of the world for girls and women.

Her work is now studied by students throughout Britain. She has given poetry readings and lectures in Europe and the United States and her work has been translated into ten languages. Gillian Clarke

DID YOU KNOW?

The Nobel Prize is awarded to persons, irrespective of nationality, who have done most in the five areas Nobel considered most important for the benefit of mankind – physics, chemistry, medicine, literature and peace.

CHECK THE NET

Gillian Clarke has her own helpful website at **www. gillianclarke.co.uk**

DID YOU KNOW?

In 1997 an anthology *Trying the Line* was published to acknowledge both her achievement and her sixtieth birthday and contained tributes from Ted Hughes and Seamus Heaney.

DID YOU KNOW?

Gillian Clarke has released an audio cassette featuring a number of her poems together with notes designed to help examination candidates.

has also written plays, has worked as an editor of *The Anglo-Welsh Review* and as a translator (from Welsh). She is also the cofounder of Ty Newydd, a writer's centre in North Wales.

Gillian Clarke has a particular interest in encouraging others to write and has acted as a tutor of creative writing to all ages from primary school children to adults. She is a frequent visitor to schools and has worked as a poet in residence at Llantarnam Comprehensive School, Cwmbran, at Radyr Comprehensive and at Cathays High School, Cardiff. Since being selected for various GCSE anthologies, and being widely studied for A level in *Six Women Poets* she has been invited more and more to secondary schools. She has read on stage with other NEAB and AQA poets at about fifty city venues a year to large gatherings of students.

Gillian Clarke has her own website which stresses that poetry is accessible. She says 'Poetry is for everyone. One of my ambitions in life is to destroy the prejudice that says that poetry is just for the few'.

She now lives in West Wales where she is more in touch with the world of nature. She lives near Carmarthen with her husband where they tend a small flock of sheep and run an organic farm.

Pre- 1914 Poetry Bank

BLAKE, WILLIAM: *The Little Boy Lost/Found*

William Blake was born in 1757 to a very poor London hosier. Apart from a brief spell in Sussex, Blake lived in or near to London all his life. He received little formal schooling, yet his work bears witness to an extremely wide range of reading: the Bible, Milton, Greek and Latin classic literature. His spiritual and intellectual development was greatly influenced by his brother, Robert, who died at the age of twenty. All of Blake's work contains an extraordinary mix of apocalyptic vision, political fervour, reworkings of Christian myth and psychological exploration. Like

Wordsworth, Blake was politically both a radical and a libertarian. He was committed to the principles of social, political and sexual equality. Blake died in 1827 and was buried in a pauper's grave.

BROWNING, ROBERT: *My Last Duchess/ The Laboratory*

Robert Browning was born in 1812 in the London suburb of Camberwell. He was the son of a clerk at the Bank of England and was extremely intelligent. In 1846, he married the poet Elizabeth Barrett in dramatic circumstances and they eloped to Italy where they lived until her death in 1861. Robert Browning returned to London with their son. Robert soon achieved greater recognition and, along with Alfred Tennyson, was regarded as the leading poet of the Victorian age. He died in 1889.

CHECK THE FILM

The classic film, *The Barretts of Wimpole Street* is based upon the relationship of Robert Browning and Elizabeth Barrett.

CLARE, JOHN: *Sonnet*

John Clare was born in 1793, the son of a farm labourer in Northamptonshire in the English Midlands. He received only a basic education and left school at the age of twelve to become a ploughboy. He also worked in a public house and as a gardener. His first collection of poems was published in 1820. It sold well and he became known as the 'Ploughman Poet' who wrote in a simple accessible way about the simple pleasures of the countryside. His subsequent publications were less popular and he fell victim to mental instability. He died in 1864.

DID YOU KNOW?

John Clare escaped from an asylum in Epping Forest in 1841 and walked 80 miles to his home surviving by 'eating the grass by the side of the road'.

GOLDSMITH, OLIVER: *The Village Schoolmaster*

Oliver Goldsmith was born into an Irish rural family, his father was a clergyman. When he went to Trinity College in Dublin he was so poor that he had to act as a servant to the more fortunate students. He started writing to try and pay his bills though he was still deeply in debt when he died in 1774. He tried his hand at every type of writing including journalism and he was admired by his contemporaries for the clarity and elegance of his expression.

DID YOU KNOW?

As well as being a writer, Goldsmith was also an able flautist.

HARDY, THOMAS: *The Man He Killed*

Hardy was born on 2 June 1840 in Higher Bockhampton in Dorset, near Dorchester. His father was a master mason and building contractor. Hardy's mother, whose tastes were literary, provided for his education and the young boy studied Latin, French and began reading widely. Between 1871 and 1897 Hardy wrote many novels set in the West Country in the early part of the nineteenth century, *Far from the Madding Crowd* (1874) and *Tess of the d'Urbervilles* (1891) being among the most celebrated. But Hardy preferred to write poetry and regarded his novels as a source of income.

JONSON, BEN: *On my first Sonne*

Ben Jonson (1572/3–1637) was a dramatist, poet, scholar and author of court masques. He was born in or near London and was educated at Westminster School. Before he became well known as a writer he was employed by his stepfather as a bricklayer, and then travelled as a soldier in Flanders where he is supposed to have killed an enemy in single combat. He also joined a travelling theatre company (strolling players).

MANLEY HOPKINS, GERARD: *Inversnaid*

Gerard Manley Hopkins was born in 1844 in Stratford, Essex, to a prosperous and artistic family. He was a highly intelligent young man and was educated in Highgate and at Oxford University. He had an intense interest in religion and eventually left the Church of England to join the Catholic Church in 1866. He became a Jesuit priest, destroying all the poetry he had already written, since he felt that poetry conflicted with his religious principles. However, as a student of Theology in North Wales he began to write again. His work though was so unusual that it was not published in his lifetime. After his death from typhoid in 1889 his friend, the Poet Laureate Robert Bridges, finally arranged the publication of his work in 1918. Since then his reputation has grown. Gerard Manley Hopkins is now regarded as one of the leading poets of his age.

SHAKESPEARE, WILLIAM: *Sonnet 130*

William Shakespeare is one of the most famous men in history and a writer of global significance. He was born in 1564 in Stratford-upon-Avon. His family was prosperous and he probably attended the local grammar school. He married Anne Hathaway who was eight years older than him and pregnant in 1582. They were to have

DID YOU KNOW?
William Shakespeare was a shareholder in the Globe Theatre that burnt down during a performance of his play *Henry VIII*.

three children. Nothing is known about the next few years of his life, though he probably joined a travelling group of actors and left Stratford. William Shakespeare wrote 154 sonnets. Some critics believe that they represent his most personal writing. They say that they are like a diary that outlines actual events in his life.

EXAMINER'S SECRET
You will not earn marks for regurgitating the life story of a writer.

TENNYSON, ALFRED: *Ulysses/ The Eagle*

Alfred, Lord Tennyson was the fourth of twelve children of a clergyman in Somersby, Lincolnshire. His grandfather had disinherited his father and he spent his early years in relative poverty. His life and work encompass most of the Victorian age and he is seen as one of the writers, along with Charles Dickens, who represent this time. He was a popular figure of national importance. Alfred Tennyson was very patriotic and both excited and disturbed by the great changes that were occurring in his lifetime. His poetic style was very conventional. He had an instinctive grasp of **rhythm** and the sound of his poems. They are ideally suited to being read aloud. This makes some of his best work very memorable.

TICHBORNE, CHARLES: *Elegy*

Tichborne was a Catholic who lost his life during the religious persecutions of the sixteenth century. It is likely that Tichborne was hung, drawn and quartered and his head displayed on a pole after the execution. Tichborne was made a Saint of the Catholic Church by becoming one of the 'Forty Martyrs of England and Wales'.

WHITMAN, WALT: *Patrolling Barnegat*

Walt Whitman was born near Huntington, New York, in 1819. His father was a carpenter. When Whitman was four years old, his family moved to Brooklyn, New York, and after attending school for six years he was apprenticed to a printer. He subsequently had a wide variety of jobs, including being a newspaper editor, a teacher and a builder, until he decided to devote the rest of his life to writing poetry. Whitman's poetry shows an assertion of the value of the individual and the connectedness of all humanity. It makes a defiant break with traditional poetic concerns and its style exerted a major influence on American thought and literature.

CHECK THE NET

http://members.aol.com/wordspage/bio.htm contains a useful Wordsworth biography.

WORDSWORTH, WILLIAM: *The Affliction of Margaret*

Wordsworth was born 7 April 1770 in Cockermouth, Cumberland. His father was a steward on a country estate and the poet's childhood was relatively hard, especially since his mother died when he was eight and his father when he was thirteen. A lonely, self-sufficient boy, it was at this time that he began to develop a fondness for the beauty and sublimity of the Lake District. Wordsworth had strong republican sympathies and was greatly influenced by the events in revolutionary France. From 1797 Wordsworth lived with his sister, Dorothy. They met the poet Samuel Taylor Coleridge, and he and Wordsworth began a collaboration that resulted in their publishing *Lyrical Ballads*.

DID YOU KNOW?

An 1899 police report described Yeats as 'more or less revolutionary'. He published 'Easter 1916' in 1916 about the Irish nationalist uprising.

YEATS, WILLIAM BUTLER: *The Song of the Old Mother*

William Butler Yeats was born in Dublin. His father was a lawyer and painter. In 1867 the family moved to London but returned to Dublin in 1881. Yeats studied at the Metropolitan School of Art and became interested in the supernatural and mysticism. He was also interested in folktales and participated in the movement for the revival of Celtic identity. He died in 1939.

Now take a break!

Romanticism

Wordsworth, Coleridge, Blake and Southey belonged to the first stage of the Romantic movement of poetry.

- The Romantics valued individual feelings and intuition above reason. Indeed they were individualists who spent more time disagreeing than collaborating with each other.

- They believed in imaginative freedom.

- They were interested in 'natural' forms of human existence, such as peasants, outsiders, children, whom they believed were uncorrupted by organised society.

- They had a strong sense of the importance of their own experience as a way to acquire insight and wisdom, so a lot of their writing is autobiographical.

- Above all, the Romantics thought that the contemplation of nature was a way of coming to an understanding of the self. Hence Wordsworth's attachment to Westmoreland, an area of great natural beauty, then, as it is now.

- In the preface to the *Lyrical Ballads* (1800) Wordsworth defines poetry as 'the spontaneous overflow of powerful feelings'. This meant that poems should shape themselves 'organically' rather than adhere to a set of pre-existing rules of composition. It also means that Wordsworth wanted to express himself in a more 'natural' language than conventional **poetic diction**, as he says 'a selection of language really used by men'. In this way Wordsworth established for the nineteenth and twentieth centuries the idea that poetry could be written using 'ordinary' language.

- They were greatly influenced by the events of the French Revolution and its consequences. They were revolutionary sympathizers but the Napoleonic wars made Coleridge and Wordsworth change their stance and they became conservative in their outlook.

PART TWO

SUMMARIES

Storm on the Island

❶ Humans prepare for a storm.

❷ The storm can neither be seen or touched.

❸ Its effects are profound.

STRUCTURE

The poem opens with a simple statement. Storms are not unusual and the people who live on the island are prepared for them. The earth is their sanctuary. They 'Sink walls in rock' (line 2) and describe the slate that roofs them as 'good' (line 2). The earth is not fertile; it is 'wizened' (line 3) and has never produced hay. At least there is no danger that this could be blown around. The wind is their enemy. The threat comes from the very air that we breathe but you cannot see it. You can only see its effects on trees, for example, but there are none on the island. As a result you cannot 'listen to the things you fear' (line 9). If there were trees you could imagine that the wind beats only them but without them the wind appears to be everywhere. There can be no escape because the air and danger are all around you.

The effects upon the sea cannot be contained either. It transforms the sea into 'a tame cat / Turned savage' (lines 15–16) The sea doesn't just beat the cliffs. The spray is thrown up on to the houses. All they can do is to 'just sit tight' (line 16) whilst they feel as if they are under attack from the wind which behaves like an enemy fighter that dives strafes and bombs.

The closing line sums up the absurdity of the situation: all that preparation, all that power, yet when all is said and done, it is 'a huge nothing that we fear' (line 19).

GLOSSARY

wizened shrivelled, dried up

DID YOU KNOW?

In the eighteenth century, French scientists believed that the wind was caused by the trees waving their branches about.

STYLE

Seamus Heaney speaks to us directly. The poem has a conversational tone as if he is by our side, sharing his thoughts: 'you know what I mean' (line 7) he says. The verse itself is broken up, reflecting the effects of the storm. Long sentences are set against short phrases. Lines 5–11 are a good example of this and can be compared with the short sentences that end the poem (lines 16–19).

THEMES

At the end of the poem we are reminded that the force of the storm is unseen. It has no substance yet it is everywhere. It cannot be touched or contained: 'It is a huge nothing that we fear' (line 19). The air is everywhere. It surrounds us. It is an essential part of life. We breathe it. Yet in a storm something turns it savage. All humans can do is to hide away by burrowing into the ground. When one element – the air – turns against us, all we can do is to take shelter inside another – the earth.

> ### CHECKPOINT 1
> How does Seamus Heaney indicate that the earth is good?

Links

Elements of air, earth and water

- Heaney's other poems

Different view of nature

- Sonnet (John Clare)

Different description of a storm

- Patrolling Barnegat (Walt Whitman)

Perch

1. Seamus Heaney watches perch swimming in the 'clear Bann River' (line 1).
2. He is aware that they inhabit a completely different world.
3. He can observe their world but never experience it for himself.

STRUCTURE

The fish swim against the current and hang stationary in it as if on a 'water perch' (line 1). They are comfortable because this is their world. They have no particular qualities. Indeed they are unexceptional. They are 'little flood-slubs' (line 3).

A slub is a thick piece in a thread or a piece of material. To Heaney these fish are like lumps in the thread of the stream. 'Slub' is a vowel away from 'slob' which suggests laziness, yet the fish can hang against the current effortlessly. They are 'bluntly holding the pass' (line 5). It is so easy for them to do this that they are 'adoze' (line 6).

PERCH

The water is their element. It is their 'finland' (line 8). This is very different from the human world, 'the fenland' (line 8). They live in a world of movement, 'the everything flows and steady go of the world' (line 10). The water is their air and they guzzle the current.

Seamus Heaney can look at their world from the outside, from the bankside, but he cannot be a part of it. He observes them 'Under the water-roof' (line 6) that is the limit of their experience. The 'finland' (line 8) is theirs, not his.

STYLE

Heaney tries through his words to repeat the experience of watching the fish in the water. He ties the poem together by using half-rhymes in each verse, apart from the middle of the poem (lines 5 and 6) where he uses 'pass' and 'adoze'. This lack of **rhyme** confirms that the perch appear asleep by breaking the **rhythm**, which in turn suggests the movement of the water.

He describes the fish carefully as 'runty' (line 3) which reflects their shape. This illustrates that the poem reflects a careful observation of nature. Seamus Heaney points out how their appearance changes as the light reflects on the water in his use of the word 'slur' (line 7).

THEMES

There is a sense of admiration and close observation in the poem which reflects the importance of the natural world in Seamus Heaney's work. What we can see is that nature serves its own purposes. It is not there to serve the needs of humans. Indeed, for the most part we can only observe.

Links

Nature

- Inversnaid
  (Gerard Manley Hopkins)
- Sonnet
  (John Clare)

Animal inhabiting its own world

- The Eagle
  (Alfred Tennyson)

Blackberry-Picking

1 Seamus Heaney remembers the experience of collecting blackberries in the late summer.

2 Every year they would collect them.

3 Every year the fruit would rot before they could use them.

CHECK THE BOOK

Seamus Heaney has said that the poet who most influenced his early style was Gerard Manley Hopkins.

CHECKPOINT 2

What do you notice about the punctuation of this poem?

DID YOU KNOW?

Seamus Heaney began teaching in Belfast. He says that many of the boys he taught went on to be active members of the provisional IRA.

DID YOU KNOW?

The poem is dedicated to Philip Hobsbaum a writer who brought together poets in Belfast to discuss their work with each other and encouraged Seamus Heaney.

STRUCTURE

The poem is set in August when the blackberries ripen. They are described with striking **imagery**. The first one to ripen is like a 'clot' (line 3) – a thickening of the blood. This reference to blood is carried through the poem and is one of the means by which Seamus Heaney links blackberry picking to other issues. They ripen gradually, changing colour and texture. They begin as a knot which reflects both texture and their tight impenetrable appearance. From inanimate knots in line 4 they soon become 'eyes' in line 15.

The first one always had an intense taste, representing the goodness of summer. This provokes an instinctive need to gather the harvest, a 'lust for / Picking' (lines 7–8). They would collect as many as they could, filling up ordinary containers with fruit (line 9). The berries are all around them and whilst they might begin by picking the under-ripe ones that tinkle in the bottom of the cans, soon they would be full of large darker ones.

DID YOU KNOW?

Blackberries are the most common fruit growing in the wild.

But the berries, which inspire such an instinctive response to gather and to hoard, contain within themselves the cause of their destruction. When they collect the fruit they also collect unwittingly the fungus that destroys them. The fungus is like a rat (line 19) that eats them, destroying all their promise: 'The sweet flesh would turn sour' (line 21). This happens every year. They need to collect the blackberries even though they know what is going to happen. They cannot help themselves in the face of such profusion. But they rot. It cannot be stopped.

They act as they do out of hope but none of us can hide from the reality of decay. Time and life can never stand still. The moment of ripeness cannot be preserved. No moment can last forever. In this way the blackberries become a **metaphor** for our lives, which must lead inevitably to death. Life, like the blackberries, contains the very thing that will destroy it. The references to blood that run through the poem suggest the loss of innocence that occurs as we grow older which can never be reversed.

STYLE

Heaney's images in this poem are based on his sensations. He recalls the thorn pricks on the hands like pepper, the taste of the berries like 'thickened wine' (line 6), their appearance as knots, the sticky hands.

The **hard rhymes** stand out amongst the rest. The **couplets** 'clot' and 'knot' (lines 3–4) and 'rot' and 'not' (lines 23–4) that end the poem give prominence to these sounds and the ideas of blood and decay.

THEMES

The blackberries release strong emotions, a lust, a need. Yet even in the pleasure of gathering there is the pain of the thorn pricks. The reference to 'Bluebeard' (line 16), a word which mirrors the sound of the word 'blackberries' (line 2), introduces the ideas of sexual awakening and death, the things that await us as we grow older.

The idea that nature is good, is bountiful, is there to support man, is shown to be false. Just as **'The Death of a Naturalist'** does, this poem shows that nature is not neat and sweet and innocent. It contains death, decay and sex. Man is an outsider who observes nature but cannot influence it.

CHECKPOINT 3

How is the fungus that destroys the berries personified?

DID YOU KNOW?
The legend of Bluebeard, a man who murders the women he marries, is based upon a Frenchman who murdered six of his seven wives. He was burned at the stake in 1440.

Links

Man and Nature
- Inversnaid (Gerard Manley Hopkins)
- Patrolling Barnegat (Walt Whitman)
- The Eagle (Alfred Tennyson)

Contrasting relationship with nature
- Sonnet (John Clare)

Nature suggesting and representing other things
- A Difficult Birth (Gillian Clarke)
- The Field-Mouse (Gillian Clarke)

Death of a Naturalist

1. Seamus Heaney would visit the flax dam to collect frogspawn.

2. He particularly enjoyed watching it develop under the guidance of his teacher.

3. However, on a return visit, he is overwhelmed by a sense of fear.

4. He feels threatened by the frogs that live there.

CHECKPOINT 4

This is a sensuous poem, using all the senses except one. Which one is missing?

STRUCTURE

The title is significant. Because of what he sees at the dam, something in him dies – his innocent uncomplicated view of nature is destroyed. Nature is not what he thought it was. Of course the reality of the flax-dam has always been there and we are shown the decay at the beginning of the poem. At this stage, though, he doesn't see it. It is just a place to collect frogspawn. He enjoys its atmosphere.

CHECKPOINT 5

Which colours are referred to in the first verse?

The flax-dam is in the middle of town, for nature is not separate from man. It is at the heart of human activity. The words that Heaney chooses define the place for us. The dam 'festered' (line 1) and the flax 'rotted' (line 3). Its own weight pushed it down into the water. The sun assists the breaking down of the vegetation and gasses are released that bubble 'delicately' (line 5). The contrast between their appearance and the reality of their unpleasant smell is at the heart of the poem – that behind the appearance of things there lurks a different reality. The smell brings the insects – the bluebottles and the dragonflies (lines 5–7)

As the material rots, the nature of the water changes. It seems to become thicker as the frogspawn develops. It is a 'warm thick slobber' (line 8).

Earlier in the year, Heaney had collected frogspawn, 'the jellied / Specks' (lines 11–12) and watched it develop. In this way he was a naturalist, watching their development in a secure and contained environment, a jampot. He has an innocent understanding of sex. This is shown in the long sentence with phrases held together by 'and' (lines 15–19). This is the sort of sentence constructed by a child. The frogs themselves change colour – a memorable detail. This is nature as it is presented in a child's text book.

The reality is presented in the second verse. It is entirely different and it is this, and his changed perception of what he sees, that kills the 'naturalist' in him.

The day is hot and the frogs are angry. What Heaney sees at the dam this time is not like anything he has seen before. The nature of the frogs has changed. We can see this in the adjectives that are used – 'coarse' (line 25) 'gross –bellied' (line 27) 'obscene' (line 29). The air is 'thick' (line 26), as if its qualities have been changed, just as the nature of the water changed in the first verse. It is the sound of the frogs that disturbs Heaney most of all. In the first verse it was the gentle buzz of the insects. In the second there is the 'coarse croaking' (line 25) and the 'slap and plop' (line 29) as they hop around that sounds like an 'obscene threat' (line 29). They sit as if ready to explode. The use of the word 'farting' (line 30) comes as a shock, emphasising the shock of what has happened. Nature is no longer easily contained. It now poses a threat. The frogs are no

DID YOU KNOW?
Flax is a blue-flowered plant cultivated for its seeds that are used to make linseed oil. A fibre is obtained from the stem which is used to make linen. Linen production was a major industry in Northern Ireland.

DID YOU KNOW?

It takes about two weeks for spawn to change into a tadpole and a further twelve weeks to evolve into a frog.

longer innocent forecasters of the weather. They are 'slime kings … gathered there for vengeance' (line 31–2) against the boy who collected the spawn.

STYLE

The first verse is similar to the image presented by John Clare in his 'Sonnet' but as the poem develops there is the sudden intrusion of a different perception. Like Gillian Clarke, he employs close and informed description of the world and relates it to other issues. This is a personal confession, reflecting upon a central incident in the poet's development and the effect that it had upon him.

THEMES

Nature does not change. What does change are the boy's perceptions of it. The frogspawn he kept in jars on the window-sill could now grab his hand. When he realises that nature is not innocent and easily contained, then the naturalist in him dies – the naturalist who collects and watches something neatly packaged in a jam jar, where sex is about daddy frogs and mammy frogs, not about the mating calls of 'gross-bellied frogs'(line 27).

Links

Nature as a metaphor to represent something else	Significant incident in a poet's past
• The Field-Mouse (Gillian Clarke)	• Mali (Gillian Clarke)
• A Difficult Birth (Gillian Clarke)	• Catrin (Gillian Clarke)

Now take a break!

Digging

① As Seamus Heaney rests in his writing he hears his father digging outside.

② He admires his skill and remembers being with him as a child.

③ His own skills, however, lie elsewhere.

④ He will earn his living with a pen rather than a spade, breaking a family tradition.

DID YOU KNOW?

Seamus Heaney says that this was his first real poem.

STRUCTURE

The first verse is a simple sentence, describing how a pen rests snugly in the poet's hand like a gun. This **simile** suggests the power of writing, that it can fire out the words that can describe the world around us. Words can also take us back in time, in the same way that what we hear and see can inspire memories.

He hears the sound of a spade being pushed into the ground (line 4) and looks down on his father working in the garden. Now he is working in flowerbeds but in Heaney's childhood twenty years earlier the work was much more serious, for he dug for the potatoes that would support his family (line 8).

His father was a skilled man with a spade who had acquired a precise and accurate technique that exposed the potatoes. At this time Heaney worked with his father, helping to collect the potatoes 'Loving their cool hardness in our hands' (line 14). He was part of a family tradition, for his grandfather was also highly skilled.

Now Heaney's mind goes even further back in time, to consider his grandfather. He cut the peat that kept the family warm. The sloppy way that he took him his milk (line 20) is contrasted with the neat precision of his work. It was work that kept him in touch with the earth (line 23). This is emphasised by the single word sentence 'Digging' (line 24) that repeats the title.

As he remembers this, his other senses are re-awakened. He remembers the smell and the sound of the work:

DID YOU KNOW?

Peat is organic material found in marshy ground composed of partially decayed vegetation. It is an early stage in the formation of coal. It is cut, stacked and burnt as fuel.

CHECKPOINT 6

What does the pen become in the last verse?

The cold smell of potato mould, the squelch and slap
Of soggy peat, the curt cuts of an edge (lines 25–6)

Heaney's skills, however, lie elsewhere. He cannot hope to emulate men like these. He will have to use his skill with his pen.

STYLE

This is a simple poem but highly effective in the way in which it expresses deep respect for the skills of his family. Digging is an apparently simple task but they performed it with rhythm and precision. The poem starts with **rhymes** and the second verse, with 'sound' (line 3) 'ground' (line 4) and 'down' (line 5), takes him back into the past. These are simple memories expressed in simple sentences like line 16: 'Just like his old man'.

The repetition in the first and last verses ties the poem together. These are the thoughts that flooded his mind at this moment when he rested in his writing.

THEMES

There is a sense of community here and perhaps an indication that Heaney feels he has somehow disappointed his family. A tradition has been broken: 'But I've no spade to follow men like them' (line 28).

Links

Poet travels back in time to bring the past alive in the present

- Cold Knap Lake (Gillian Clarke)
- Catrin (Gillian Clarke)

References to the past

- My Last Duchess (Robert Browning)
- Ulysses (Alfred Tennyson)

Sense of admiration

- The Village Schoolmaster (Oliver Goldsmith)

Mid-Term Break

❶ Seamus Heaney is unexpectedly called away from school.

❷ At home he finds the family in considerable distress.

❸ His younger brother has been killed in a car accident.

STRUCTURE

A mid-term break should be a happy occasion but this is not. It is
not a holiday shared with the other pupils. Heaney is in fact
separated from them, as if the school is not quite sure what to do
with him. Something has happened that has made him different. He
is put to wait in the college sick bay all morning, as if he is ill,
waiting to be collected. He accepts what is happening to him without
comment. Indeed he does not offer any personal comments at all. He
speaks to us in simple uncomplicated sentences as if numbed by
events: 'At two o'clock our neighbours drove me home' (line 3).

A mood has already been created, for the bells marking the change
of lessons 'knell' (line 2), suggesting funeral bells. The second
suggestion that something might be wrong is that his neighbours,
not his parents, take him home.

When he arrives home he finds himself in an unusual situation, for
his father who 'had always taken funerals in his stride' (line 5) is
clearly distressed and greets him at the porch. As he moves further
into the house we see that the event has brought the whole
community together. 'Big Jim Evans' (line 6) is there along with the
old men who want to shake the young Heaney's hand. The only one
who doesn't understand is the baby who laughs in innocence. The
poet is aware that his status has changed, for his elders express how
sorry they feel. As a child the men would not normally treat him
with such deference. Heaney is still a child though and holds on to
his mother's hand as she 'coughed out angry tearless sighs' (line 13).

In line 15 we are told what we have already suspected. There has been
a death and the body is brought home in an ambulance that evening.

DID YOU KNOW?
Seamus Heaney was
a boarding student
at St Columb's
College in Derry
when his brother
Christopher died.

The next morning Heaney is taken up to the room where he sees the body of his brother, who he last saw six weeks ago before he went away to school. The snowdrops and the candles create a peace and calmness around the body that is so different from the circumstances of his death. His brother is paler now, but apart from 'a poppy bruise on his left temple' (line 19) his body is unmarked, for the car that killed him didn't run over him, it knocked him away. The box he is in, his coffin, is like the cot he once slept in. It is 'a four foot box, a foot for every year' (line 22).

STYLE

CHECKPOINT 7

There is one full rhyme in the poem. Where is it and what is its effect?

There is no rhyme scheme here nor any complicated imagery. It has a simplicity in its word choice and in its sentence length. Yet it is undeniably a poem. The line endings and the separation into verses are deliberately chosen to give emphasis to particular ideas. The whole piece is carefully and artfully constructed.

The first line ends with 'sick bay'. Whilst Heaney is waiting there, his brother is in hospital. One brother is brought home alive by neighbours. The other is brought home dead in an ambulance. His father he believed to be strong is 'crying' (line 4). A neighbour says that it was 'a hard blow' (line 6) for the family, which suggests the blow that killed his brother. The only mark on him is the bruise that his brother appears to be 'Wearing' (line 19) as if he had any choice about it. This is a striking image. The use of 'poppy' in the same line suggests the colour of the bruise and also remembrance.

The poet observes the incident. Of course the baby does not understand what has happened but the poet as a young boy seems shocked, unsure how to react, embarrassed by the concerns of the old men. He says nothing. His father and his mother cry, the neighbours talk, the baby laughs but Heaney makes no sound. He watches silently and we watch with him.

THEMES

This is a poem of immense power, a power that emerges from the use of very simple language. It is the ordinariness of the words that speaks to us and makes the poem very moving, the simple language matching his simple childhood impressions. Much of the power of the piece comes from the idea of a child trying to understand the death of another child.

CHECKPOINT 8

What two types of flower are referred to and what effect do they have?

Links

Attitudes to death

- Tichborne's Elegy (Charles Tichborne)
- My Last Duchess (Robert Browning)
- The Laboratory (Robert Browning)

- On my first Sonne (Ben Jonson)
- The Man He Killed (Thomas Hardy)
- October (Gillian Clarke)

Follower

1. Seamus Heaney remembers the skill his father displayed when ploughing.

2. As a child he hoped to emulate him.

3. Now, though, their roles have been reversed and his father has come to rely on him.

STRUCTURE

The father's presence seemed to fill the child's world, emphasised by the word 'globed' (line 2). The reference to the sail stresses his strength. It was clear to the poet even then that his father possessed great skill. He was an 'expert' (line 5). He controlled his team of horses easily, working neatly and precisely 'Mapping the furrow exactly' (line 12).

The young poet followed his father, stumbling over the uneven ground created by the ploughing. It has been turned so easily that the earth seemed 'polished' (line 14). He remembers how his father

 CHECK THE FILM

Watch Pete Postlethwaite as Mr Jones ploughing at the start of the film *Animal Farm* by Jim Henson's Creature Shop (1999) and see ploughing done badly!

would carry him on his shoulders and how he moved to the rhythm of his father's pace, 'Dipping and rising to his plod' (line 16).

At that time his desire was only to emulate his father's skill. He was Heaney's role model. He would follow him around, watching him carefully, the way he would 'close one eye' (line 18). Perhaps in doing so he was in the way, 'a nuisance, tripping and falling' (line 21), talking constantly, but he wanted to learn and acquire these skills that he found so impressive. When he tried to follow though he stumbled. His path through life will have to be a different one.

Their roles have now reversed. As his father has grown older, he has lost much of his physical certainty. Whereas before it was the poet who stumbled, now it is his father. When he was a child the father accepted responsibility and 'rode me on his back' (line 15). Now it is the child's turn. He cannot escape from his responsibility to look after the man who was once so precise and assured:

> It is my father who keeps stumbling
> Behind me, and will not go away.   (lines 23–4)

He does not seem to accept that responsibility quite so readily.

DID YOU KNOW?

Ploughing, turning the soil over for planting, is one of the world's oldest farming operations.

STYLE

The poem has a traditional regular rhyme scheme. Each verse is a self-contained unit ending in a full stop, apart from a run-on between verses two and three which suggests the movement of the ploughing team as it moves backwards and forwards across the field. The poem is written in the past tense until we reach the last verse which tells us about what is happening now. What we ask ourselves when we consider the title is whom does it refer to? The poet or his father? The fact is that each generation is replaced by that which follows. The passage of time cannot be prevented. Nothing ever stands still.

THEMES

This is another poem that speaks of the importance of the earth. Like much of Heaney's poetry it begins with a simple statement that places the poem in a place and a context. It is a poem about his father and once again, as in 'Digging', he emphasises his skill and expertise.

Heaney reflects upon his own experience and his own past in the same way that Ulysses does in Alfred Tennyson's poem. Like Ulysses, he does not feel either capable or ready for the life mapped out for him by tradition. He wants something more. Heaney has turned his back upon the soil, for he has no skill in the areas that have sustained his family for generations.

> ### CHECKPOINT 9
>
> In lines 17 and 18 we are told that the young poet copied his father. Which lines describe those actions of his father that he tried to copy?

Links

Sense of admiration

- Cold Knap Lake (Gillian Clarke)
- The Village Schoolmaster (Oliver Goldsmith)

Close relationship between father and son

- The Little Boy Lost/Found (William Blake)

- On my first Sonne (Ben Jonson)
- Catrin (Gillian Clarke)
- The Song of the Old Mother (W. B. Yeats)

At a Potato Digging

1 Seamus Heaney watches men at work harvesting the potatoes behind a digger.

2 This leads him to consider the ravages of the nineteenth-century potato famine.

STRUCTURE

The first line places the poem firmly in the present: 'A mechanical digger wrecks the drill' (line 1). The word 'wreck' is an important one. It suggests farming on an industrial scale. It lacks the precision shown by earlier skilled men like his father, whose abilities were presented to us in **'Digging'** and **'Follower'** Here the potatoes are thrown up out of the ground (line 2). All the men need to do is collect them.

They are not, though, described as men. They 'swarm' (line 3), they are like 'crows' (line 5). Heaney watches their movements. They are stretched out across the field and seem to be servants of the machine, their heads bowing almost in worship. They hope that the machine that reveals the potatoes will keep the famine away and so they will serve it.

The hard physical labour of bending and picking is described. The earth is the 'black / Mother' (lines 11–12) who gives them life. This is another poem by Heaney in which the earth is seen as a vital life-giving element. Nourishment will emerge from it and the workers live in fear that the 'black / Mother' might turn against them once more. So their act of homage is repeated every year and the ground they turn over becomes like an altar before which they bow and upon which they offer the potatoes that are revealed, to keep the 'famine god' (line 14) away.

In the second section the potatoes are described. They are like stones and they live in the earth as stones do. Heaney points out their contradictions. They are like pebbles. They are white like 'flint' (line 17). Stones of course carry no nourishment, but the

CHECKPOINT 10

What do you notice about the image used in line 10?

? DID YOU KNOW?

When the potato was first introduced to America in 1719 it was planted in Londonderry New Hampshire.

insides of the potatoes are 'white as cream' (line 23). They are the 'petrified hearts' (line 22) of the potato drills, the reason why the drills exist. They have eyes (line 21). This takes us on to their description as 'live skulls' (line 29), an image that suggests their colour, and links with the idea of eyes. But this carries a warning. Their eyes were once 'slit' (line 21). Now they are 'blind' (line 29).

These **images** are repeated at the very start of the third section but their effect is completely different. A **rhyme** scheme is reintroduced as Heaney now takes his poem into the past, to the Irish Potato Famine of 1845–7. Suddenly the images he used now refer to men. They are:

> Live skulls, blind eyed, balanced on
> wild higgledy skeletons (lines 30–1)

desperately searching for food. They did not use a mechanical digger. They 'scoured the land' (line 32).

They are famine victims. They eat the diseased potatoes with the desperation of animals. They 'wolfed the blighted root and died' (line 33).

Now the potatoes do not have the permanence of stone. They do not have purity. They putrefy. The earth in which they were stored in clamps turns against them. It no longer brings life as it did before. Now from the earth there emerges death. The clamp where they are stored is no longer a 'hutch' (line 19); it is a 'pit' (line 36), a word which suggests a grave.

The rotting of the potatoes brings about the rotting of the people (line 37). Heaney now describes their suffering, their physical changes as the famine victims starve. Their eyes die. They no longer have their humanity. They are like plants. The earth that can give life is now 'the bitch earth' (line 43). Their hope has disappeared, 'rotted like a marrow' (line 45). Decay, part of the natural process, previously enriched the earth ('humus', line 25). Now decay rots and destroys: 'Stinking potatoes fouled the land' (line 46). The potato pits are now like grave mounds.

 DID YOU KNOW?
The potato was brought to Europe from South America by the Spanish in the sixteenth century.

 DID YOU KNOW?
Blight is a disease caused by a fungus *Phytophthora infestans* and devastated the Irish potato harvest between 1845 and 1847.

The vocabulary in this verse is striking – 'fouled' (line 46), 'pus' (line 47) 'filthy' (line 47) and 'sore' (line 49). These words form the atmosphere of desperation, of how the earth turned against those who depended upon it. The line between life and death is a narrow one. The things that brought life can just as easily take it away. When the earth turns against us, we die. The potato pickers cannot escape the fear that it might happen again.

The final part of the poem brings us back into the present. The pain of hunger had been like a beak in the victim's guts (line 41). Today the birds are scavenging whilst the workers, tired by their hard physical labour, stop for lunch. The **rhythm** of their lives is emphasised by the certainty of the rhyme in the first verse. They eat their lunch gratefully. They are exhausted but they are pleased. They have a harvest.

The doubt, however, is always there. The ground is 'faithless' (line 56). The blight could return and devastate their lives once more. So their careless spills are like an offering to god to help the famine stay away.

STYLE

The metrical arrangement of the poem serves to underline the poem's meaning. In the first section, set in the present, there is a clear pattern representing the steady repetitive nature of their work. Such regularity does not re-appear until the last section when the rhythm is broken in the last line to give emphasis to the offering. It is their desperation that makes them hope that such an offering of crumbs will keep the famine away.

The second section is much freer, perhaps suggesting the way the potatoes are scattered across the ground. Section three has a different rhyme pattern. Each of the verses is made of complete sentences, ending in a full stop. These are not opinions. These things are certainties. The uncertain restoration of the rhyme reflects their changed relationship with the earth.

DID YOU KNOW?

In New York State a law has been passed which requires every school to teach students about the Irish Famine of 1845–7.

CHECK THE NET

Search for 'Irish famine 1845–7' to learn more about it.

THEMES

Trust is an important part of any relationship. The potato blight destroyed that trust between humans and the earth that sustains them. The earth is one of the essential elements of life upon which humans depend. But the earth, like the air in **'Storm on the Island'**, could turn against them. It has done before. They can never forget that the famine could emerge from the ground again.

> **DID YOU KNOW?**
>
> Seamus Heaney objected to his inclusion in the 1982 *Penguin Book of Contemporary British Poetry* in verse:
>
> 'Be advised, my passport's green.
>
> No glass of ours was ever raised
>
> To toast the Queen'

Links

Telling a story

- The Laboratory (Robert Browning)
- My Last Duchess (Robert Browning)

Imagery and narrative construction

- On the Train (Gillian Clarke)

Importance of the past

- Ulysses (Alfred Tennyson)
- Catrin (Gillian Clarke)

 **Now take a break!**

TEST YOURSELF (SEAMUS HEANEY)

FROM WHICH POEM?

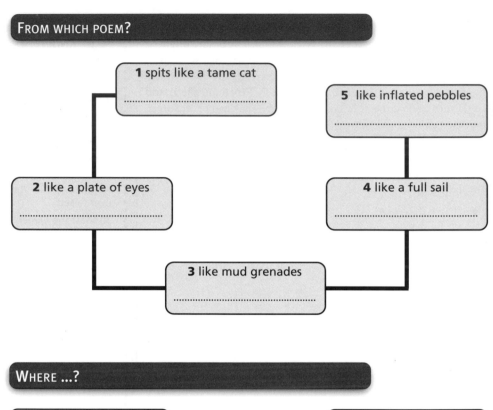

1 spits like a tame cat

....

5 like inflated pebbles

....

2 like a plate of eyes

....

4 like a full sail

....

3 like mud grenades

....

WHERE ...?

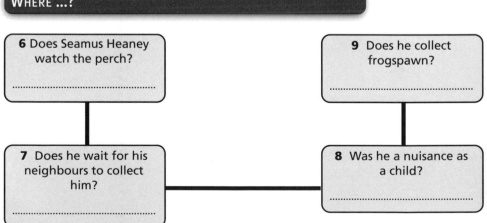

6 Does Seamus Heaney watch the perch?

....

9 Does he collect frogspawn?

....

7 Does he wait for his neighbours to collect him?

....

8 Was he a nuisance as a child?

....

Check your answers on p. 140.

Catrin

1. Catrin asks to stay out playing in the street for a little longer.
2. Gillian Clarke reflects upon the nature of her relationship with her daughter.
3. She thinks back to her daughter's birth.
4. That experience may have separated them but they remain forever joined.

STRUCTURE

As Clarke looks at her daughter who has made her request, the poet's mind goes into the past, to the moment of birth. It was the key moment in their lives when they became two separate individuals. She remembers standing at the hospital window in the moments before the birth, watching other people carrying on with their ordinary lives, oblivious to the life-changing moment that was about to happen. All they cared about at that moment were 'traffic lights' (line 5).

The process of birth set the tone for their relationship. They were still joined together physically by the umbilical cord, 'the tight / Red rope of love' (lines 7–8). What the poem shows of course is that they will always be joined emotionally. It is after all a rope of love, not of control or restraint.

The room may indeed have been a sterile hospital delivery room 'disinfected / Of paintings or toys' (lines 10–11) but it was transformed into a very personal space because of what happened in it: 'I wrote / All over the walls with my / Words.' (lines 11–13).

Birth creates two separate individuals where previously there was one, but the struggle is a tender one, because their love will always connect them. Birth is a physical separation but it is not an emotional separation.

This idea runs on into the second verse. It was not a struggle that could end in victory or defeat. It was more properly a starting point

DID YOU KNOW?

The name Catrin is the Welsh form of Catherine which in turn derives from the Greek word *katharos* meaning 'pure'.

DID YOU KNOW?

The umbilical cord attaches the unborn baby to the placenta in the mother's womb. The placenta is the organ that nourishes the baby.

in a new relationship. Clarke goes on to say that the legacy is still there, that they are still struggling. They are still joined, though the old rope now comes from the heart. And because they are entirely separate individuals the love that joins them also brings tensions – 'defiance' (line 24) and 'conflict' (line 27) – as they struggle for dominance.

Catrin asks to stay out to play for a little longer in the dark. Perhaps it is too dangerous. As a mother Clarke sees things that Catrin does not. But she also knows that Catrin is growing and is trying to assert herself. She also knows that however much any of us believes that we are free, 'that old rope' (line 25) ties us to our family.

STYLE

The poem has at its heart a woman's experience, the effect and the resonance of childbirth. It is the process of childbirth that fills the first verse, enriching the language. There is reference to the umbilical cord, to the pain and joy of labour, to the blood in the lines 'coloured the clean squares / With the wild tender circles' (lines 13–14).

The vocabulary of the poem is strong, suggesting the dynamics of the relationship that began at this moment. Words like 'confrontation' (line 7), 'Fought' (line 9), 'struggle' (line 15), 'shouted' (line 16), 'Defiant' (line 24), 'Tightening' (line 26), 'conflict' (line 27) make sure that the poem avoids any sentimentality. The hospital room became a 'glass tank clouded with feelings' (line 19), the real feelings of real people.

THEMES

This is a very powerful poem that has at its heart the image of love as a rope that binds, that replaces the physical joining that exists before birth. The sense of family is important throughout Clarke's work as we see in '**Mali**', where Catrin has a daughter of her own.

CHECKPOINT 11

Why do you think there is no reference to Catrin's father in this poem?

Links

Parents

- Follower
  (Seamus Heaney)

- The Affliction of Margaret
  (William Wordsworth)

- On my first Sonne
  (Ben Jonson)

Time and memory

- Ulysses
  (Alfred Tennyson)

- Death of a Naturalist
  (Seamus Heaney)

Baby-sitting

❶ Whilst baby-sitting, Gillian Clarke becomes aware that the strength of her feelings for her own children cannot be transferred to any other.

❷ Another woman's child could never accept her as their mother.

STRUCTURE

The poem begins with two short complete sentences. They contain negative words – 'strange', 'wrong', 'don't' – words not normally associated with babies. Clarke is baby-sitting, with a baby-sitter's responsibilities but not a mother's responsibility: 'I don't love / This

DID YOU KNOW?

Gillian Clarke says that her readers show her meanings in her work that she previously missed herself.

CHECKPOINT 12

Of the five senses, two are not mentioned in the poem in relation to the baby. One is taste. What is the other? Why do you think it does not feature?

baby.' (lines 2–3). The maternal bond does not exist. The child is 'perfectly acceptable' (line 5), a measured and rather distant description that contrasts with the emotional content of **'Catrin'**. This is because love is not there. In fact Clarke is afraid of her, afraid of what she might do because she is not the mother and cannot act as a mother should. If she wakes, there will be no love. Rather, there will be hatred and there will be little that she can do to placate her. Her own feelings too will be unhelpful: 'the perfume / Of her breath will fail to enchant me' (lines 9–10). A mother accepts and recognises her own child unquestioningly, but another person cannot. The fact that the child is not given a name stresses the absence of this bond.

The second verse goes on to examine the baby's feelings. She will feel completely abandoned. The strength of this feeling is established by the word 'Abandonment' (line 12) at the start of a line with a capital letter and by the repetition of the 'ab' sound from the previous word 'absolute'. She will feel that she will never see her mother again. Clarke now identifies two different life crises that older people face and suggests that the baby's pain will be greater than either the pain of abandonment by a lover or the pain of bereavement (lines 12–16). The mother is the child's world, the source of comfort and nourishment (line 18). If the baby wakes, though, all she will find will be Clarke, the baby-sitter. However much she cares, she can never be the mother. The truth of this is made emphatic by the repetition in the last line of 'It will not come' (line 20).

STYLE

The poem is enriched by close observation. It is clear that Clarke knows what babies are like. There is no romanticism at all and Clarke speaks directly – 'her nose / Will stream disgustingly' (lines 8–9). She writes candidly of her own feelings in clear simple language. The images she chooses though are powerful – 'hot midnight rage' (line 8), 'bleached bone' (line 16) – which reinforces the lack of that sentimentality which is often associated with babies. We can also see how Clarke avoids **rhyme** but instead draws upon an old Welsh poetic tradition of using regular lines with clear **assonance**. This is a

DID YOU KNOW?

The first recorded use of the term *baby-sitter* is found in America in 1937. The verb *to baby-sit* did not appear for the first time until at least ten years later.

feature of much of her work. In addition to the examples already given, look at the use of the 's' sound through the poem.

THEMES

What Clarke explores here is an essential part of the human condition, the instinctive nature of the relationship between parents and their children. This features in a number of her poems selected here, from '**Mali**' to '**The Field-Mouse**'.

Links

Motherhood	Fatherhood
• Catrin (Gillian Clarke)	• On my first Sonne (Ben Jonson)
• The Affliction of Margaret (William Wordsworth)	• The Little Boy Lost/Found (William Blake)

Mali

1 Gillian Clarke writes about the emotional bond that exists between a woman and her children.

2 It is inspired by the birth of her granddaughter, Mali.

STRUCTURE

On the occasion of her granddaughter's third birthday, Clarke thinks back to her birth and to the effect that this event had upon her. It re-awakened in her the strong emotional bond that exists between mother and child. She had thought that these feelings had gone forever and she is surprised at their resurgence as another generation is born: 'that unmistakable brim and tug of the tide' (line 2) is an important **metaphor** for these feelings.

The sea is always an important **image** for Clarke. The tidal flow and its connection with the phases of the moon suggest a woman's

 DID YOU KNOW?
The moon does not just influence the tides. A full moon can also induce labour because of the effect it has on amniotic fluid.

DID YOU KNOW?
Amniotic fluid is the water-like fluid that surrounds the baby in the womb.

menstrual cycle and her fertility, something that for her now lies in the past. It is an image that also carries with it a suggestion of the sea of amniotic fluid in which the baby still lives. Like the tide, maternal feelings have returned, washing over her once more.

She remembers the day of the birth, rushing through the 'summer lanes' (line 4) whilst everyone else is going about their daily lives, oblivious to the importance of this occasion. There is an important link here to the birth of Catrin, when she watched cars at the traffic lights. Now Catrin is about to become a mother herself. For others life goes on. People drive slowly, cows block the road (lines 5–7).

The second verse begins a long sentence that does not end until line 16 with the words 'harvest moon'. The times of the year are important to Clarke, as we see in **'October'** and in **'A Difficult Birth'**. Here it is the edge of summer and autumn when fruits ripen, like the apples and the blackberries (lines 11–12). The child too is ripe, and arrives easily. It might be the wrong place but it is the right time, for just like the fruits they have been picking, it is ready.

We can see a contrast here with Seamus Heaney's **'Blackberry-Picking'**, where the fruit leads to decay. Here it precedes birth.

The reference to 'harvest moon' (line 16) repeats the significance of the moon and the tides and stresses the importance of the natural cycles that lead to harvest and birth. The next day three generations of females gather under an umbrella as a family. Clarke is 'life-sentenced' (line 20), for nothing can ever break these ties that have formed through birth. Even the sea, for which she says she has a great affinity, 'could not draw me from her' (line 21).

DID YOU KNOW?
A harvest moon is a full moon that occurs around the end of September. Traditionally it was believed to help the ripening of corn.

In the final verse we return to the present. The birthday cake she bakes looks like a home, the centre of the family. A new generation revives the 'old trees' (line 23) so that they appear to blossom once more. The connection between Clarke and the old trees is clearly implied. They are a unit, a family that shares the same blood. Blood is frequently a negative image, associated with death and destruction. But is also part of the process of birth, a positive, central human experience. We see this in 'Catrin', to which perhaps this poem is a companion piece. We can see too the absence of such 'blood' in 'Baby-sitting' and what affect that absence has. Here they celebrate the birth with blood, the family blood that unites the generations. Mali herself is associated with the great natural force of the sea and that image is used as a blessing from these women who represent three drops of the same blood to which, perhaps, another generation will not be added.

STYLE

Like 'Catrin' the poem moves backwards and forwards through time in order to show how essential human bonds are formed. Clarke examines her own feelings and responses on the occasion of becoming a grandmother, reflecting upon a woman's experience.

THEMES

The idea of the sea runs through the poem. The great natural forces of the tide and the moon are forever associated with the birth of Mali. She is part of it, part of the natural rhythm of the seasons. She came from water, from the amniotic fluid that was her world. She will take her place as the new generation, as the third drop of blood. As trees and hedgerows bring fruit, as a diary herd produces milk, so a woman gives birth. The links with Clarke's other work in this selection are obvious in their focus on family and upon the natural cycles of birth and death.

> **DID YOU KNOW?**
> Mali is a Welsh name, a form of Mair or Mary, equivalent to the English name Mollie.

> **CHECKPOINT 13**
> Why are their fingers purple in line 12?

Links

Relationship between the generations

- Ulysses (Alfred Tennyson)
- Digging (Seamus Heaney)
- Follower (Seamus Heaney)

Other family relationships

- The Song of the Old Mother (W. B. Yeats)
- The Affliction of Margaret (William Wordsworth)

A Difficult Birth, Easter 1998

1 An old ewe experiences difficulties in giving birth.

2 This is connected with the Good Friday peace negotiations in Northern Ireland.

3 Gillian Clarke helps to deliver the lamb.

4 She is surprised when a second lamb appears unexpectedly.

STRUCTURE

As usual with Clarke, the first sentence clearly establishes the context of the poem. An old ewe is about to give birth for the first time. This is a **metaphor** for the emergence of a peace agreement in Northern Ireland (line 3). After a long and barren time, there is to be new birth, a new chance for life. It is, however, a time of tension in Belfast and on the farm. The ewe is 'serious, restless and hoofing the straw' (line 4). Celebrations are put on hold until the difficulties have been resolved, an obvious reference to both events.

The birth of the lamb is a difficult one, the labour long and painful just like the negotiations in Belfast, a city that has been in labour for the birth of peace for 80 years. The waters around the lamb, the 'salty ocean' (line 8), broke some time earlier. There seems no possibility of a successful unassisted birth so her husband, to whom the poem is addressed, phones for professional help (line 13).

Clarke is aware that when professionals are called, 'the whitecoats' (line 15), they patronise women and bring technology with them. They use 'their needles and forceps' (line 16), not trusting to nature but relying on man-made tools. Perhaps they are not needed; perhaps problems can be resolved without male-orientated intervention. It is after all a female occasion, as we have seen in 'Catrin' and 'Mali'. So, acting as a midwife, she inserts her hands and eases the lamb out 'in a syrupy flood' (line 21). The two females, the woman and the ewe, work together to ensure a successful birth. They do not need male help with their patronising attitude and their equipment. All that is needed are hands. So they

DID YOU KNOW?

The word 'lamb' comes from the Greek word for 'deer'. No one knows why.

CHECKPOINT 14

What is the image in the second verse that connects this poem to **'Mali'**?

'strain together' (line 19) and when her husband appears the drama is over and they are peaceful.

There could have been a death (line 22) but instead, as in Northern Ireland, there is new life. There is, though, a further surprise. A second lamb is born to this previously unproductive ewe. Clarke links this to the Easter story, to the Resurrection, a symbol of hope. This is a clear reference to the peace deal and after all the drama the poem ends on a moment of hope.

CHECK THE NET
Search for 'history of Northern Ireland' to learn more about the troubles and the Good Friday peace agreement.

STYLE

This is a masterful poem, full of connections and cross-references, full of resonance. The birth of lambs on Good Friday, both of them important Christian **symbols**, is linked to the delicate peace negotiations. Both need help; both processes, peace and birth, are exhausting, 'tamed by pain' (line 10). The poem moves smoothly between the births and the political events, indicated initially by the title, which emphasises these connections.

It is invested with the close observation that you would expect of a sheep farmer. We see the restless ewe, 'hoofing the straw' (line 4) and sipping the amniotic fluid (line 8). When the suffering ewe lies down, all Clarke can see are 'Two hooves and a muzzle' (line 12). The connections between these two initially disparate events are striking. Ireland is like the ewe, old, barren and tired. Suddenly on Good Friday there is the promise of new life. Everything could have gone wrong. The lamb could have died, the peace process could have collapsed but 'the stone rolled away' (line 24) just as the stone had rolled away from Christ's tomb, indicating his resurrection.

DID YOU KNOW?
Christ is also known as 'The lamb of God'.

THEMES

The huge significance of birth that we have seen in **'Mali'**, **'Baby-sitting'** and **'Catrin'** is explored once more. Any birth is difficult and painful – whether human, animal or political – but remains a positive life-giving experience. Here human affairs are linked with the natural world in a direct way.

> ## Links
>
> ### Birth and parenthood
> - Mali
>   (Gillian Clarke)
> - Baby-sitting
>   (Gillian Clarke)
> - Catrin
>   (Gillian Clarke)
>
> ### Links between home life and world events
> - The Field-Mouse
>   (Gillian Clarke)
>
> ### Human involvement with nature
> - Digging
>   (Seamus Heaney)
> - At a Potato Digging
>   (Seamus Heaney)
>
> ### Death
> - The Man He Killed
>   (Thomas Hardy)
> - On my first Sonne
>   (Ben Jonson)

The Field-Mouse

❶ The accidental death of a field-mouse is linked to the suffering caused by civil war in central Europe.

❷ Gillian Clarke reflects upon the vulnerability of children who suffer in such conflicts as the mouse did in the field.

STRUCTURE

The poem is placed immediately in context. It is summer and the hay is being cut. This, though, is a modern poem. Instead of the humming insects that we see in John Clare's **'Sonnet'**, here there are 'jets' and the radio carries 'terrible news' (lines 1–4). This is not a traditional image of summer. It is a blade that we see, that cuts and harms (line 6). The grass is like 'a snare drum' (line 1) an image that has military connotations. However, the neighbouring farmer is fertilising his land with lime, some of which drifts over the hedge, 'a chance gift of sweetness' (line 9). He is doing what his land needs, but it is also benefiting Clarke's land too. This shows that people are inter-connected, that each individual's actions can affect someone else.

CHECKPOINT 15

What two weapons are referred to in this poem?

The second verse examines the consequences of the tractor blade. The idea of death and destruction is established immediately in the first line with the reference to 'the killed flowers' (line 10). In one field there is life and fertility. In the adjoining field there is pain and death.

Death touches the children. They find a field-mouse, fatally injured in the haymaking. It is quivering but is still has the light of life in its eyes. They know, however, that it will not survive, for it is consumed by pain 'big as itself' (line 14). This mouse becomes a symbol of the suffering in civil wars in central Europe. There it is people who are in pain. Even children cannot be protected from it. The last line of the verse indicates that all are implicated in the use of the word 'we' (line 18) when she says 'staring at what we have crushed'.

Once the hay has been harvested it now becomes a killing field and the garden is like a refugee camp 'inhabited by the saved' (line 20). The work in the field may have finished but in Europe the suffering continues. In the night Clarke is haunted by an image of the vulnerability of children. The 'dance in the grass' (line 24) exposes them, whereas before, in verse two, they knelt in the security the grass provided. Now they are vulnerable, for the protecting grass has gone. In an arresting image they are shown to be as fragile as 'mouse-ribs' (line 25). She hears gunfire. Her neighbour who was previously blessing her land with drifting lime is now 'wounding my land with stones' (line 27), exchanging fertility for barrenness.

STYLE

The poem begins with simple statements that establish the context. What underlines the poem is the sense of responsibility and the idea that individual actions can have consequences for others. It explores such consequences in three equal verses. In the first verse it is the unexpected kindness of the gift of lime that brings fertility to her land. In the second verse it is the death of an innocent field-mouse as a consequence of haymaking. As Clarke points out in the third verse, we can turn our backs on the news but we cannot make it go away.

CHECK THE BOOK
The first chapter of *Daniel Martin* by John Fowles is an excellent description of hay-cutting.

DID YOU KNOW?
The field-mouse is largely nocturnal. It is about 9 cm long with an 8 cm tail. It feeds on seeds and grain.

CHECKPOINT 16
What unites the two references to the media?

CHECK THE NET
A good place to find about the history of the former Yugoslavia is **www.bbc.co.uk**.

THEMES

By our actions we make our children vulnerable, destroying the bonds that Clarke's other poems have established. We must take responsibility for what we do, for none of us is separated from our neighbours. We have responsibilities. We must show a concern for others.

The poem suggests the collapse of Yugoslavia into smaller states, full of refugee camps, with neighbours who had once been supportive turning fertile ground into a land of stones.

Links

Relationship with natural world
- A Difficult Birth (Gillian Clarke)
- Sonnet (John Clare)
- Inversnaid (Gerard Manley Hopkins)

Death and nature
- Death of a Naturalist (Seamus Heaney)
- At a Potato Digging (Seamus Heaney)

War poem
- The Man He Killed (Thomas Hardy)

 DID YOU KNOW?
Gillian Clarke says 'Trust your response. Trust that idea that hops into your mind'

October

1 A close friend dies during October.

2 Clarke considers her own mortality.

3 She stresses how important writing is to her.

STRUCTURE

The title places the poem at a specific time of year. It is mid-autumn. Mali was born in late summer. Now the year has moved on and the fruitfulness of late summer has turned to decay.

The first image in the poem – 'a dead arm in the bright trees' (line 2) – suggests a death amongst the living. It is perhaps part of the natural rhythm of the world. Leaves change colour, die and then fall. Plants too are changing colour. They are 'more brown now than blue-eyed' (line 6). The stone lion, a garden ornament, changes colour in the autumn rain and the lobelia that surrounds him has changed too. As it dies back it has become matted and tangled, a wet mane turned into dreadlocks.

The reason for this succession of gloomy images is now clear. Her friend has died and is to be buried. The men carry her coffin which is light, 'lighter / than hare-bones' (lines 8–9). The air seems to weep like the mourners and their faces are stony, like the face of the lion in the first verse. We feel the rain, we see the grief and now we hear the flowers falling into the deep grave.

We are told in the last verse that the effect of her loss is to make Clarke write. It is hard to come to terms with the death of a friend. She herself is perfectly well but 'For a while health feels like pain' (line 14). She becomes aware of her own mortality, realising that there is so much that she wants to do, so many details of the world she wants to capture in words – 'that robin's eye / in the laurel' (lines 16–17). So she must write frantically, 'like the wind' (line 18) trying to hold back time, to live beyond the day ordained for her death.

CHECKPOINT 17

What does the broken branch in the first line represent?

 DID YOU KNOW?

Lobelia is a garden plant with small blue, scarlet purple or white flowers. Some varieties are reputed to have medicinal qualities.

DID YOU KNOW?

Orcop (line 7) is in Herefordshire, close to the Welsh border.

STYLE

The elements are strongly expressed in this poem, particularly the air and the wind which as a force breaks branches, makes trees tremble. At the funeral, the air seems to weep in sympathy. Afterwards the wind is seen as a creative force that she must emulate in her writing. Whether it is out of a fear of death or a fear of the loss of time, there seems to be a creative spur as a consequence of the funeral.

THEMES

Death in this poem is a natural occurrence, a part of life, in the same way that October is a part of the cycle of the seasons. Our relationship with unexpected or untimely death, however, is always going to be different.

Links

Attitude towards death

- Tichborne's Elegy (Charles Tichborne)
- Mid-Term Break (Seamus Heaney)

War

- The Man He Killed (Thomas Hardy)

Murder

- My Last Duchess (Robert Browning)
- The Laboratory (Robert Browning)

DID YOU KNOW?

This poem has not been published elsewhere. Its first appearance was in the AQA Anthology.

On the Train

1. Clarke travels home to Wales by train on the day after the Paddington rail crash in October 1999.

2. She considers the pain of families caught up in the crash.

3. She tries to phone home but no one answers.

STRUCTURE

The first verse of the poem describes an ordinary train journey. The movement of the train as it sways suggests that Clarke is cradled, an **image** of comfort and security. The fields may be flooded after rain but she is safe listening to her music (line 2). But already there is a sense of apprehension. The Walkman is described as a 'black box' (line 3), the name given to flight recorders which are always sought for after a plane crash. The tea in the cup 'trembles' (line 4) with the movement of the train, but also perhaps with fear. Clarke thinks of the security of home and of family.

The second verse moves back to the previous day and switches to other families who have had this security taken away from them. She writes of ordinary families in the suburbs leading their ordinary lives, listening to radios, taking their children to school, going off to work. They are leaving their homes, which represent to them just the same security that Clarke's home represents to her. They do not know that their train is leading them to death, to 'the blazing bone-ship' (line 12).

One of the abiding memories for rescue workers at the site of the disaster is of all the mobile phones ringing in the wreckage as people frantically tried to contact loved ones. Clarke builds in the mobile phone message they may have heard at the very start of the third verse. They cannot make contact any more. The repetition of 'calling later' (lines 15–16) reflects the repeated calls that are made. Clarke draws a parallel between the rubble of the crash site and the emotional devastation as those at home, in 'suburban kitchens' (line 17), realise how much their lives have been touched. The disaster reaches out and intrudes into their homes in the same way as a phone call. The verse ends with a powerful line. Wolves inspire fear and attack man, 'howl' (line 18) suggests grief and 'silent telephones' (line 18) reminds us that they will never be answered.

In the final verse the poem returns to the present journey, along the route the fatal train took the day before. Clarke phones home and there is no answer. It is probably just a temporary inconvenience, which contrasts with the devastating permanence of the previous

DID YOU KNOW?
More than thirty people died and many more were injured on 5 October 1999 when two trains collided after one passed through a red light at Paddington Station London.

DID YOU KNOW?
One of the trains was travelling from South Wales to London.

CHECKPOINT 18

What does the use of the mobile phone offer?

day's events. In the circumstances, though, she needs the comfort of home. Like others, she objects to the use of mobile phones, but today she is prepared to be more tolerant. A banal mobile phone call would be reassuring in the aftermath of the train crash. Of course in normal circumstances such a message would indeed be reassuring. But in the changed circumstances following the crash the message could also create anxiety. Perhaps yesterday doomed passengers also called to say 'Darling I'm on the train' (line 26).

STYLE

This is a carefully crafted poem. It is balanced, with the two middle verses dealing with the events of the previous day and the first and last verses dealing with the present. It succeeds through its **imagery** of creating an impression of fear and threat in the mind of the reader. The phone is the central image. Suddenly banal phone calls have meaning, are welcomed, are vital. Yet the messages themselves have not changed, only the context. So when she phones to offer reassurance she could **ironically** be creating the very anxiety she is trying to allay.

THEMES

What is particularly effective in the poem is the use of phrases from everyday speech. These serve to stress how the disaster affected ordinary lives. It is another example of how Clarke finds her inspiration in the domestic world that we all inhabit.

Links

Movement between past and present	Use of narrator
• Mali (Gillian Clarke)	• My Last Duchess (Robert Browning)
• Catrin (Gillian Clarke)	• The Laboratory (Robert Browning)
Life-changing events	• The Man He Killed (Thomas Hardy)
• Mid-Term Break (Seamus Heaney)	

Cold Knap Lake

1 Clarke remembers her mother who once resuscitated a child who had fallen into a lake in Barry.

2 When the child is taken home she is beaten by her parents.

3 This memory makes her consider the passing of time.

STRUCTURE

The poem begins with a simple clear sentence. It is unambiguous, unadorned. The statement suggests that the child is already dead, which is reinforced by the **images** at the end of the verse. The child is 'Blue lipped' and covered in weed, 'dressed in water's long green silk' (line 3).

The child is revived by Clarke's mother who breathed life back into the child through mouth-to-mouth resuscitation. For her this is one of the roles of women, to give life, on this occasion to a stranger's child. There is a pause, the crowd stand by watching, 'drawn by the dread of it' (line 10). A crowd of people can do nothing. An individual woman can give life.

Suddenly the child breathes, 'bleating' (line 11) like a lamb. This image suggests Christ. Like Jesus, the drowned child has been reborn. She is no longer blue-lipped. Now she is 'rosy' (line 12). Clarke's father takes her home where the parents, in their relief, beat her for getting into difficulties. There is a clear contrast between the actions of a stranger who gives life back to a child and the father who punishes her. A stranger can do this but cannot have that emotional bond that we see in **'Catrin'**, **'Mali'** and also in **'Baby-sitting'**. Yet this father thrashes his daughter 'for almost drowning' (line 14).

It was indeed a memorable event. Clarke's mother was a heroine, giving life as she once did through birth, but this time to a stranger's child.

In the last two verses this memory gives the poet an opportunity to reflect. It is fixed in the past at a particular time just after the war,

CHECKPOINT 19

What do you notice about the length of the verses in this poem?

 DID YOU KNOW?

Cold Knap Lake is a local beauty spot in Barry, South Wales, where Gillian Clarke was brought up.

for her mother is in 'a wartime cotton frock.' (line 7). What other events are there in her past that she has forgotten about, into which new life may be breathed? The poem ends in a **rhyming couplet** which connects the incident at the lake with other memories from her childhood. She questions whether she was really there. Memories can be dredged from the past just as elegant swans can churn up the mud with their webbed feet as they glide upon Cold Knap Lake. Lots of things exist under the surface of memory 'where satiny mud blooms in cloudiness' (line 18). Sometimes the water closes over the top of them just as it did over the girl. But sometimes memories, like her, can be revived.

DID YOU KNOW?

This is a personal memory, rather like Seamus Heaney's **'Mid-Term Break'**. See how the tone of these two poems is very different.

STYLE

Again Clarke draws her inspiration from her own experiences and examines her past and the effect that has had upon her. Such memories can free themselves from the past. Like swans they can be churned up and suddenly released, flying gracefully.

THEMES

A number of the themes of Clarke's work appear in this poem. It presents another memorable event taking place in the everyday world, as we saw in **'Mali'** and **'Catrin'**. This time a child is brought back to life in front of an audience. It focuses again upon the role of

the woman who gives life, as Clarke did in **'A Difficult Birth'**. All the father can do is to beat the poor child.

Links

Memory and the past

- Tichborne's Elegy (Charles Tichborne)
- Ulysses (Alfred Tennyson)

Parents and children

- Little Boy Lost/Found (William Blake)
- Digging / Follower (Seamus Heaney)
- On my first Sonne (Ben Jonson)

EXAMINER'S SECRET

Don't look for unusual or 'clever' links between poems. Such comparisons will be hard to sustain throughout a whole essay.

Now take a break!

TEST YOURSELF (GILLIAN CLARKE)

FROM WHICH POEM?

1 Environmental blank, disinfected

....

2 hot midnight rage

....

3 We thought her barren

....

4 the star goes out in its eye

....

5 the slow / fall of flowers

....

6 Too soon to phone

....

7 The crowd stood silent

....

8 an umbrella on the beach

....

IN WHICH POEMS?

9 car lights

....

10 traffic lights

....

11 a wartime cotton frock

....

12 newspapers

....

Check your answers on p. 140.

BEN JONSON, 1616 – On my first Sonne

1 The poet bids farewell to his seven-year-old son who has died.

2 He feels that he has is being punished for expecting too much of the boy.

3 He wishes that he could cease to feel as a father and wonders why people lament the dead when they should be envied.

4 At least his son, having died so young, has avoided all the misery that life can bring.

5 He bids his son rest peacefully. The boy will be known as Ben Jonson's best piece of poetry.

6 From now on, Jonson will never become too attached to anything he loves.

 DID YOU KNOW?
Jonson was tried at the Old Bailey for murder for killing fellow actor, Gabriel Spencer, in a dual in the Fields at Shoreditch. He escaped the gallows only by pleading benefit of clergy.

STRUCTURE

The poem is an **epitaph**, or **elegy**, which was a common poetic form in Jonson's time.

There are twelve lines of **rhyming couplets** divided into three sections.

 DID YOU KNOW?
Wordsworth wrote three essays on epitaphs. Yeats actually composed his own epitaph at the end of his poem 'Under Ben Bulben'.

In the first four lines, after the poet has bid his son farewell, he tries to find some meaning for his loss. These lines promote the idea that the boy's death is somehow the result of Jonson's pride, his possessive ambition for his son's future. The child had only been 'lent' (line 3) and after seven years it was time to 'pay' him back.

In the next four lines Jonson questions his own grief. He asks why we should lament the enviable state of death when the child has escaped suffering and the misery of ageing. He cannot answer this question.

The final four lines resolve the situation. He asks that the child, or perhaps the maker of the gravestone, record that this boy was Jonson's 'best piece of poetrie' (line 10), his proudest creation. He concludes by vowing that he will be more careful with those he loves; wary of liking and so needing them too much.

CHECKPOINT 20

How do we know that Ben Jonson regards his son as more important than his work?

STYLE

Jonson's poetic language can be described as strong and vigorous, virile. Read the poem aloud in the voice you think Jonson might have used – phrases such as 'O, could I lose all Father, now' (line 5) have a directness and emotional honesty that are very typical of the poet. There is no elaborate **imagery**; the **metaphor** of the boy's life as a loan – 'Seven yeeres tho' wert lent to me, and I thee pay...' (line 3) is simple and everyday.

This style or **tone** of writing owes much to the Latin classical poets: Catullus, Martial, Horace, while at the same time it is not far removed from colloquial English.

Epitaphs

Epitaphs were commemorative verses appearing on tombs or written as if intended for this appearance; they were tributes to the dead. This form seems to suit the best features of Jonson's style, with its **decorum**, clarity, proportion and classical form.

THEMES

Ben Jonson wrote this elegy after the death in 1603 of his eldest son, Benjamin, aged seven. The theme is simple and universal: a father's grief at the death of a young son.

DID YOU KNOW?

Ben Jonson and John Donne, each in his own way, represented a revolt against the traditions of Elizabethan poetry. The result was decisive for the future of English poetry. Jonson contributed a strong sense of formal classicism. Donne extended the possible range of allusions in poetry, i.e. the kind of things that could be referred and written about.

Links

Death and children
- Mid-Term Break (Seamus Heaney)
- Cold Knap Lake (Gillian Clarke)

Death and duty
- The Man He Killed (Thomas Hardy)

Death as necessity
- My Last Duchess (Robert Browning)

W. B. YEATS, 1899 – The Song of the Old Mother

1 The 'Old Mother' describes how she gets up at dawn to light the fire and then works all day until night time, cleaning and cooking.

2 She describes the young in the family, asleep in their beds dreaming of trivial things. During the day they devote their time to idleness.

3 She states that she herself must work until she grows old and dies.

STRUCTURE

The structure of this poem is simple: a ten line single verse comprising of five rhyming couplets.

STYLE

'The Song of the Old Mother' comes from a collection of romantic poems called *The Wind among the Reeds* (1899). There is a certain

DID YOU KNOW?

The 'Old Mother' could represent the mother of all Ireland, or perhaps a previous, more responsible generation.

song-like lilt to the rhythm of the poem, especially in the use of 'And' (lines 3, 5, 7, 8, 10) which reinforces the apparently endless toil of the woman's life. 'Musical' language is used too – Yeats had a tremendous ear for **assonance** and **alliteration**. Pick out some examples and consider the effect they are meant to have – is Yeats interested in sound for the sake of sound, or does the particular sound of the language reinforce an idea? Notice the way Yeats repeats the phrase 'seed of the fire' (line 2) in the last line but with different adjectives attached to it. Why?

CHECKPOINT 21

How does the **metre** contribute to the effect of this poem?

THEMES

The theme is simple like the language and structure of the poem. Since Yeats was interested in Irish folk culture, he was concerned to express what he believed were the emotions of the peasant population.

> **Links**
>
> **Changing parental responsibility**
>
> - Follower (Seamus Heaney)
>
> - Catrin (Gillian Clarke)
>
> - Ulysses Alfred Tennyson

EXAMINER'S SECRET

When quoting poetry, the best technique is to 'integrate' the quote with your comment. (Like the word *integrate* in the last sentence.)

WILLIAM WORDSWORTH, 1807 – The Affliction of Margaret

❶ A mother laments the loss of her son. She asks where he could be and what has happened to him.

❷ She has not seen the boy, her only child, for seven years. To be constantly hoping to see him again and yet to be continually disappointed is hellish.

❸ He was a beautiful, well-born boy. She sent him away an honest, innocent and confident person. Children do not realise how much power they have to upset their mothers, but this does not reduce the parent's love.

④ She refuses to continue to be self-pitying, even though she feels neglected and has shed many secret tears over the boy.

⑤ She asks her son not to be afraid to return to his mother, especially if he has been brought down in the world.

⑥ She regrets that people do not have wings like birds so that after they have wandered in the world they can return home quickly.

⑦ Perhaps her son is being cruelly treated in a prison. Perhaps he is in some distant land being attacked by lions. Perhaps he has drowned at sea.

⑧ All this talk about the dead communicating with the living is a lie. If it was true, she would have heard from the one she longs for so much.

⑨ Her doubts multiply. Everything upsets her. No one understands. If anybody happens to feel anything for her, it is only pity. She wishes you would come back to her, because he is her only friend in this world.

CHECK THE FILM

Pandaemonium directed by Julian Temple (USA Films, 2001) is a visually dazzling, thoughtful and intelligent film that shows how Coleridge and Wordsworth were once the equivalent of rock stars in their day.

STRUCTURE

Eleven seven-line stanzas. The poem begins with the question from which the whole piece develops – 'Where art thou...?'. Each stanza is devoted to an aspect of the woman's psychological situation, culminating in the final desolate conclusion of the last verse, 'Beyond participation lie / My troubles...' (lines 71–2).

STYLE

Although formal in design, this monologue uses the first person to create the illusion of a personal statement, an expression of profound loss. This is an 'illusion' because Wordsworth's diction and syntax are obviously that of a poet and not an actual speaking person. Notice the way 'poetic' diction is mingled with the rhythms and tone of everyday English: 'beauteous' (line 16), ' blasts of heaven' (line 44) and 'Wellborn. Well bred' (line 17), 'I dread the rustling of the grass' (line 65).

GLOSSARY
participation help/ support

'The Affliction of Margaret' is based on the case of a poor widow who lived in the town of Penrith, near the poet's home at Grasmere. Her sorrow was well known. She kept a shop, and when she saw a stranger passing by, she was in the habit of going out into the street to enquire of him after her son.

CHECKPOINT 22

Lyrical Ballads appeared in 1800. It was headed by a preface in prose that constituted Wordsworth's manifesto for a new **naturalism** in English verse. What evidence can you find in **'The Affliction of Margaret'** of Wordsworth's approach to poetry writing?

THEMES

The woman's 'affliction' is not merely the loss of her son, but not knowing what has happened to him: the unbreakable bond that a mother feels for her child.

The poem focuses on the woman's present feelings, and only fleetingly refers to the story of how she 'sent him forth' (line 17) into the world. Why do you think this is?

Links

Maintaining family bonds
- Follower (Seamus Heaney)
- Mali (Gillian Clarke)
- Catrin (Gillian Clarke)

Breaking bonds
- My Last Duchess (Robert Browning)
- The Laboratory (Robert Browning)

WILLIAM BLAKE, 1789 – The Little Boy Lost/Found

1 A little boy loses his way while following his father.

2 He finds himself lost in the dark night.

3 God appears to him looking like his father.

4 God leads him to his mother who is searching for him.

STRUCTURE

The shortness and simplicity of these two poems make them easy to memorise. They are obviously matched and should be read 'side by side': the turning point in the 'story' comes at the last line of **'The Little Boy Lost'**, 'And away the vapour flew' (line 8).

CHECK THE BOOK

As well as being a poet, throughout his life William Blake worked as a professional artist and engraver. He illustrated several editions of his own poems such as *The Book of Thel* and *Songs of Innocence*.

STYLE

Both poems have simple **diction** and syntax. The style is direct, almost childlike, yet weighted with a visionary effect. The vapours disappear and the boy is led by 'the wand'rng light' (**'The Little Boy Lost'** line 2) to God who replaces the father figure as a true protector of the child.

CHECK THE NET

William Blake on the web: **http://www. betatesters.com/ penn/blake.htm**

THEMES

The link between parents and a child is the focus, yet, typically, it is difficult with Blake's poems to identify a straightforward theme. He makes simple things and situations carry a lot of meaning. The two poems could make up a little **allegory** of a Christian or visionary nature in which goodness and innocence are restored.

Links

Vulnerability of children
- The Field-Mouse (Gillian Clarke)

Childhood innocence
- Death of a Naturalist (Seamus Heaney)

CHARLES TICHBORNE, 1586 – Tichborne's Elegy

DID YOU KNOW?

Tichborne's real name was not Charles but Chidiock!

❶ Tichborne was one of many Catholics who lost their lives during the religious persecutions in the sixteenth century.

❷ In the first verse the poet lists all the good things in his life which have changed by his situation – youth, joy and hope.

❸ The second verse alludes to the irony of his early death, of a life hardly lived and to his forthcoming execution.

❹ The last verse confronts the inevitable, death, and implies that all people must die one day.

STRUCTURE

Each line expresses an aspect of his existence contrasted with the pain of the present. Each verse ends with same line, like a **refrain**. In structure, it is very well crafted. The 'refrain' is integrated to underline what the poet has said in each verse.

STYLE

The tone is regretful and very sad. In each line the quality named in the first half is negated in the second. For instance, in the first stanza,

DID YOU KNOW?

Quite a lot of poetry was written in the Tower at this time (1586), as Catholics, especially priests, were the prey of Queen Elizabeth's officers. The captives were generally tortured in the Tower, then hung, drawn and quartered. It was a common sight to see the head of such a victim displayed on the railings after the execution.

'prime of youth' is contrasted with a 'frost of cares' (line 1). The contrast is between two unlike things – 'prime' (literally spring) and 'frost' (standing for winter) – making the comparison particularly stark. Another contrast, 'corn' / 'tares' (line 3) – alludes to a parable found in the Christian Bible. The corn represents those who will be 'saved' and go to heaven; the 'tares' are the damned that will burn in hell.

The poet makes us feel the despair in the poem, by his use of repetition. Some of the contrasts, notably those in lines 5, 11 and 17 are not contradictory statements at all, but paradoxes related to Tichborne's early death. In fact they are true when examined closely:

'The day is past, and yet I saw no sun'   (line 5)
'My thread is cut, and yet it is not spun'   (line 11)
'My glass is full, and now my glass is run'   (line 17)

Many of the contrasts are **metaphors** or instances – 'My thread is cut' (line 11), which uses the visual image of a severed thread of cotton to represent the ending of his life by death.

Even though the use of contrast is very conventional, Tichborne endows the writing with great sadness and regret through his use of **imagery** and through his **tone**. There is no bitterness or resentment in his voice, only a kind of weary acceptance of his fate. Naturally,

CHECKPOINT 23

Does the fact that this poem is in the 'true' voice of the poet make any significant difference to how you read it?

GLOSSARY
tares an injurious cornfield weed

CHECKPOINT 24
Some people might find Tichborne's elegy for himself a little mechanical, self-pitying even, in the way it is laid out in **antithetic parallelisms**. Do you agree?

because we know that this fate was real and did take place, this adds a special poignancy to the poem. You should look at how the **rhyme** and the **rhythm** in the poem help communicate this feeling of regret.

THEMES

The main idea is that, in the face of his coming execution, Tichborne feels that his life is over without his having really lived it. (He was twenty-eight.)

Links

Inexorable progress of time

- Ulysses (Alfred Tennyson)

- October (Gillian Clarke)

Casual approach to death

- The Laboratory (Robert Browning)

- My Last Duchess (Robert Browning)

Death in war

- The Man He Killed (Thomas Hardy)

THOMAS HARDY, 1902 – The Man He Killed

1 A soldier reflects on the man he has killed in battle. If they had met in some other context, such as an inn, they would have sat down and drank together.

2 But lined up face to face as enemy soldiers, they shot at one another, and the speaker killed the other man as he stood in line.

3 The reason the speaker shot at him was because he was his 'foe' (line 10).

4 But probably their reasons for enlisting in the army were similar, just as casual and practical, such as being unemployed and poor.

⑤ **Yes, the speaker concludes, war is very strange: it makes you kill someone who, if you met him in a bar, you would buy a drink, or lend 'half-a-crown' (line 20).**

STRUCTURE

A simple, formal structure of five short stanzas rhyming ABAB. The last two stanzas take up the original idea of the men being equal and potential friends. Stanzas two and three set out the qualifying circumstances that change everything for the men's fate: they are soldiers in opposing armies and therefore enemies.

STYLE

Hardy imitates the speech rhythms and **diction** of an ordinary working-class man in the process of reflecting on the tragic circumstances that have made him kill someone very like himself. The quotation marks within which the poem is placed remind us that this is the direct address of a man possibly engaged in conversation with a friend after the war.

'I shot him dead because – / Because he was my foe' (lines 9–10) and '– just as I – / Was out of work' (lines 14–15) capture his doubtful, faltering attempt to rationalise what happened. There are **colloquialisms** such as 'Off-hand like' (line 14) which provide an earthy **realism** along with the rough sounding **metre**.

THEMES

At the end of the nineteenth century, Hardy published *Poems of the Past and Present* (August, 1901) a few months after the death of Queen Victoria, containing elegies and war sonnets written in 1899 on the occasion of the Boer War. This is one of those poems. All Hardy's writing is underpinned by a strong sense of the way men and women struggle against the fate that seems to govern their lives and against which they are seemingly powerless. This fate, or force, is indifferent to human suffering. It creates situations that are full of disappointment and **irony**. Consequently, Hardy's work can be seen as **tragic**. 'The Man He Killed' is a poem that dramatises one of the tragic ironies that govern Hardy's universe: men are

 DID YOU KNOW?

After his first wife died, Hardy composed some of his greatest love poems for her, even though by the end they were barely on speaking terms. He married his secretary, Florence, in 1914, a woman thirty-nine years younger than himself. Apparently, she was a very melancholy person!

CHECKPOINT 25

How would you read the line 'Yes; quaint and curious war is!' (line 17)?

---

basically the same, have the same desires and needs, yet fate in the form of society turns them into murderous enemies.

With its spareness of **metre** and diction, its use of colloquialisms, and formal structure, **'The Man He Killed'** bears comparison with the contemporary poems you are studying.

Links

Death not as a duty

- On my first Sonne (Ben Jonson)
- Mid-Term Break (Seamus Heaney)

- October (Gillian Clarke)

Narrative technique

- Compare with Robert Browning

WALT WHITMAN, 1856 – Patrolling Barnegat

DID YOU KNOW?

Barnegat Bay is on the coast of Ocean County, New Jersey

① The poem describes the sensations of a storm at midnight at Barnegat Bay.

② The first four lines introduce the reader to aspects of the sound of the storm – 'Shouts of demoniac laughter...' (line 3).

③ At line 4 the three elements of this particular storm are identified: 'Waves, air, midnight, their savagest trinity lashing'.

④ From line 5 to the final line there is a description of the scene 'Out in the shadows...' (line 5) on the shore, where 'A group of dim, weird forms...' (line 13) is patrolling the shoreline looking for signs of a shipwreck.

STRUCTURE

'**Patrolling Barnegat**' has the same number of lines as a **sonnet**, but with all lines **rhyming** alike. What makes it difficult to understand at first is the fact that it is written in one continuous sentence. Each line piles up more and more detail of a single 'timeless' experience.

The sensation of being *within* a storm is more important to Whitman than any structuring of the experience in conventional poetic form. The use of a single, rhyming present continuous verb at the end of each line gives the sense of time slowed down, so that the reader feels disorientated, dizzy with sensory overload.

But take out the main grammatical skeleton,

EXAMINER'S SECRET
Choose the questions that you have most information on and can write most about. Allocate enough time for each question.

- 'Out in the shadows...' (line 5)

- 'Where...' (line 6)

- 'A group of dim, weird forms...' (line 13)

- 'watching' (line 14)

and it's easier to see how Whitman has structured the poem, making the suspended appearance of the 'watching' (line 14) figures on the shoreline especially dramatic.

STYLE

Like much of Whitman's poetry this poem is not simple, in spite of his claim in the preface to *Leaves of Grass* that his new style was to be 'democratic' and straightforward. At first it seems as if the long **cadenced** lines have to be taken in one breath. But note that most of

DID YOU KNOW?
Walt Whitman worked as a volunteer nurse during the American Civil War.

CHECKPOINT 26

Onomatopoeia is a common feature of poetic language. Try to find some examples of it in **'Patrolling Barnegat'** and explain the effect it has.

the lines contain an implied pause. Line 5 for example gives first a place – 'Out in the shadows there' – followed by what is happening – 'milk-white combs careering'. These slight breaks become more obvious if you read the poem aloud. They help build a tremendous rhythm, giving the effect of Whitman wanting to embrace the whole experience of the storm in a series of labouring breaths.

A prominent feature of **'Patrolling Barnegat'** is the dramatic use of alliteration. The 'S' sound is taken from the key words in line 1, 'storm' and 'sea', and then repeated so that it becomes a motif that dominates the whole poem. Notice also how Whitman repeats certain phrases: 'milk-white combs careering' (lines 5 and 12), 'slush and sand' (lines 6 and 10). Why do you think the use of repetition is a technical feature of the poem generally?

THEMES

In 1855 Whitman issued the first of many editions of *Leaves of Grass*, a volume of a new kind of poetry considerably different to the conventional verse he had previously written. In this book Whitman praises the human body and glorifies the senses. **'Patrolling Barnegat'** uses an extraordinary range of sensory language. The poem seems to be contrasting the power ('That savage trinity', line 14) of the storm to overwhelm the senses and potentially destroy the indistinct 'warily watching' (line 14) human figures.

Links

Another storm
- Storm on the Island
  (Seamus Heaney)

Nature
- Inversnaid
  (Gerard Manley Hopkins)

- Sonnet
  (John Clare)

WILLIAM SHAKESPEARE, 1609 – Sonnet 130

1 William Shakespeare refuses to compare the woman he loves with other things as some poets do.

2 She cannot gain in beauty as a result of elaborate comparisons.

3 For him she is perfect as she is.

STRUCTURE

The poem begins with an unambiguous statement – one that would have surprised Shakespeare's contemporaries. They expected sonnets to contain elaborate comparisons. William Shakespeare rejects this. Obviously the sun is brighter than her eyes (line 1), obviously coral is a brighter shade of red than her lips (line 2).

Similarly he points out in line 3 that her breasts are flesh coloured. They are not white like snow. How can they be?

In line 4 he asks how it is possible to compare hair with golden threads – 'wires' – when her hair is black. He has seen roses 'damasked' (line 5) – or dappled – but he does not see anything like this in her cheeks.

He continues his objection to artificiality and false comparisons by saying that her breath is not always perfumed. Whilst he loves to hear the sound of her voice he knows that music 'hath a far more pleasing sound' (line 10).

William Shakespeare has never seen a goddess so he is not sure how they walk but he knows that 'My mistress when she walks treads on the ground' (line 12).

It is in the couplet that ends the sonnet that he states his purpose in writing this poem. The woman he loves is a real woman, not a false creation formed from exaggerated comparisons. He loves her for what she is and he doesn't have to play the games of poets to prove it.

CHECK THE NET
There are hundreds of websites devoted to William Shakespeare. Some are more reliable than others. A very comprehensive website is **www.shakespeare-online.com**.

DID YOU KNOW?
A modern reader will see 'wires' (line 4) as a thread of metal. To an Elizabethan though it would mean fine gold threads that were woven into expensive hair nets.

CHECKPOINT 27

Would someone who received a poem like this feel pleased with what it said about them?

DID YOU KNOW?

William Wordsworth said the sonnets revealed Shakespeare's intimate thoughts. 'With this key Shakespeare unlocked his heart'.

CHECK THE FILM

Shakespeare in Love gives a very detailed impression of an Elizabethan theatre. Oscar winner Judi Dench was so impressed with the theatre they built that she accepted the set instead of a cash payment for her part in the film.

STYLE

He composes his expression of love by following the accepted formula for a sonnet that gives it a regular pattern and **metre**. In the first **quatrain** (i.e. the first four lines) he has one comparison in each line. In the second and third quatrains he expands his descriptions to two lines each. Then the final couplet establishes the purpose of the poem.

THEMES

William Shakespeare mocks other poets who exaggerate their lover's attributes through extravagant **similes** and **metaphors**. Love does not need such things in order to be real. Women do not need to look like something else to be beautiful. He believes that he is being more honest by rejecting such comparisons that detract from her essential humanity. Line 12 which ends his objection to falsehood is the key to the whole poem.

He himself has shown honesty in line 8 where he uses the word 'reeks', an unexpected word in the context of a poem about the poet's love. This is clearly an example of poetic honesty.

Links

Craft of writing
- Digging (Seamus Heaney)
- October (Gillian Clarke)

Sonnet form
- Sonnet (John Clare)

Rejection of artificiality
- Poems of Seamus Heaney
- Poems of Gillian Clarke

Now take a break!

ROBERT BROWNING, 1845 – My Last Duchess

① The Duke of Ferrara, during a pause in dowry negotiations, takes an envoy to see his art treasures.

② Jealous and possessive, he had his first wife murdered.

③ He shows the envoy her picture.

STRUCTURE

We are drawn immediately into the poem because it appears that the Duke is speaking to us directly. We discover later that he is speaking to the envoy of a count whose daughter he hopes to marry. He speaks with admiration of a painting of his late wife by Fra Pandolf. He admires the technique and skill (line 3). It is almost as if she is real (line 4). He invites the envoy to look at the picture closely (line 5). The artist has captured a startling likeness and remarkable facial expression (line 8).

The Duke says that whenever he allows strangers to see it they comment upon this expression, this 'spot / Of joy' (lines 14–15). As he talks though his real feelings emerge, disturbing and vicious. It was not just her husband who could bring this look to her face (line 14).

He regarded his wife as too independent, too free spirited. The expression on her face may merely have been provoked by something the artist said (lines 16–20). In fact, she was too easily pleased:

> She liked whate'er
> She looked on, and her looks went everywhere.
> (lines 23–4)

She took pleasure in everything around her at the court but this to the Duke seemed to devalue his family, for she did not seem to appreciate the honour of being married into it.

> As if she ranked
> My gift of a nine-hundred years old name
> With anybody's gift.   (lines 32–4)

? DID YOU KNOW?

Ferrara is in northeast Italy, about 80 km from Venice.

? DID YOU KNOW?

Robert Browning's wife, Elizabeth, was a much more popular poet than Robert during their time together.

CHECKPOINT 28

Do you think that the Duchess tried deliberately to upset her husband?

My Last Duchess continued

EXAMINER'S SECRET

Don't waste time trying to learn long quotations. Short ones are much more effective. A good quotation to learn for the examination would be 'I gave commands' (line 45).

She did not focus her attention upon him sufficiently. He says he was unable to make clear to her the nature of her shortcomings (line 37). It was not his responsibility to correct her or teach her, 'I choose / Never to stoop' (lines 42–3). The Duke was far too proud for this. Compromise for him would be like stooping, bringing him down to what he perceived as her level.

It became clear to him that she was not treating him with the respect he deserved because of his family and name.

> Oh sir she smiled, no doubt
> Whene'er I passed her; but who passed without
> Much the same smile?   (lines 43–5)

It could not go on. He tells us quite calmly but in a chilling inhuman moment 'I gave commands' (line 45).

The Duke did not have to do anything himself. Other people carried out his instructions for him. She was murdered.

CHECKPOINT 29

Why would the Duke want to give the impression of being thoughtful?

She should have known instinctively what to do and it was not his place to correct her, since she did not know she was imperfect. So he replaced her with a painting that could be admired and which would never change. His wife is now as he prefers her, a picture, a possession.

He suggests to the envoy that they rejoin the rest of the group downstairs (lines 47–8). This reminds us that we are listening in to a conversation. Clearly this visit to the picture has served whatever purpose it had. He is confident that the Count, whose daughter he now wishes to marry, will offer him a suitable dowry. When he says 'his fair daughter's self…is my object' (lines 52–3) we are not inclined to believe him, particularly as it comes immediately after a reference to a financial settlement. Also the use of the word 'object' is revealing. It has a double-edged meaning, for he indeed reduced his first wife to an object. This is emphasised as they go down stairs when he refers to another piece of artwork: 'Notice Neptune …Taming a sea horse' (lines 54–5). It is a possession to be proud of, to be valued. There is no sense of horror of what he has said to the envoy as he returns to where he started, talking of craftsmanship and ownership.

DID YOU KNOW?

A dowry is money or property given to a husband by his new wife's family on their marriage.

DID YOU KNOW?

Robert Browning's poem is based upon real events. Duke Alfonso II of Modena and Ferrara (1559–97) married the first of his three wives, Lucrezia de Doctors (the 'last duchess' of the poem) at Ferrara In June 1558. Lucrezia died four years later. Alfonso's second marriage in December 1565 was to Barbarian, Archduchess of Austria. She died in 1572. Alfonso's last wife (married in 1579) was Eleonora Gonzaga. She outlived Alfonso and died in 1618.

STYLE

Robert Browning's great achievement in this poem is that he reveals so many possibilities by the simple technique of allowing a character to speak for himself. The reader feels as if they are being spoken to directly and so is drawn into the events as they are being described. The power of the poem – and its ability to shock – comes from its directness. It is written in **rhyming couplets** but it has the energy and flow of ordinary speech. His use of **enjambment** means that the **rhymes** rarely fall at the end of a sentence and we thus listen to what sounds like a real conversation.

He speaks in a casual conversational tone that contrasts with the horror of what he has done. To the Duke it appears absolutely acceptable. His wife was an object and when he became dissatisfied he disposed of her and decided to get a new one. He has turned her into a picture that is much easier to control. He alone can pull back the curtain in front of her.

CHECKPOINT 30

Why would the Duke keep the picture behind a curtain?

THEMES

Lots of possibilities emerge as we piece together the story. Is he an older man trying to keep a young spirited woman in order? Perhaps she was a lively interesting woman loved by her servants as a breath of fresh air in the stifling self-important formality of the court.

DID YOU KNOW?

Elizabeth Barrett was an invalid who spent most of her life in her room under the control of her domineering father. Robert Browning and Elizabeth conducted their courtship largely by letter.

Perhaps life with the Duke was boring. Perhaps the Duke believed her enjoyment of life lay in flirtation; perhaps he feared she was unfaithful. Certainly he did not approve of her behaviour. It was not his responsibility to correct her. So he had her killed.

Why does he tell the envoy these things? Is it because he sees nothing wrong in the murder of his wife? Or is it a subtle warning about how he expects any new wife to behave? Like Neptune he will have to tame her and he expects to succeed. The hesitations in his speech – 'how shall I say?' (line 22) – 'I know not how' (line 32) – give him an air of bewilderment. How could these things happen? It is a puzzle to him. He presents himself throughout as a reasonable man of taste and refinement married to a young woman who lacked discrimination. The words he uses too are significant. Notice that her behaviour does not upset him or irritate him; it 'disgusts' him (line 38).

Robert Browning's poem suggests all these things, and more.

Links

Characters and narrative

- The Laboratory
  (Robert Browning)

- The Affliction of Margaret
  (William Wordsworth)

- Ulysses
  (Alfred Tennyson)

- The Man He Killed
  (Thomas Hardy)

Contrasting technique and purpose

- Death of a Naturalist
  (Seamus Heaney)

- Mid-Term Break
  (Seamus Heaney)

- At a Potato Digging
  (Seamus Heaney)

- On the Train
  (Gillian Clarke)

- The Field-Mouse
  (Gillian Clarke)

ROBERT BROWNING, 1845 – The Laboratory

1 A woman consults an apothecary to obtain poison in order to murder a rival.

2 She takes great pleasure in watching its preparation.

3 She is determined to enjoy her revenge.

STRUCTURE

The subtitle – Ancien Régime – places the poem in the past, in eighteenth-century France. The formal world of a royal palace is suggested. But beneath that suggestion of privilege and order there lurks hatred and revenge.

Notice how the title is an integral part of the poem, for it tells us where the scene is taking place. The speaker, a woman, ties on a mask to watch the preparation of a substance in an apothecary's laboratory. She takes pleasure in watching the procedure with its 'faint smoke curling whitely' (line 2). The last line of the first verse comes as a shock to us. It is not what a reader would normally expect from a poem. It is dramatic and arresting: 'Which is the poison to poison her, prithee?' (line 4). The line also tells us that it is being prepared for an identified victim.

In the second verse we begin to see why. The reason is revenge, for the speaker has been betrayed by her lover. She knows that he is with another woman and that they believe she has run off to cry in an empty church.

But she is not in a church praying to God. As she told us in the first verse, she is in 'this devil's-smithy' (line 3). She can hear them laughing at her. But she is much stronger than they think. Her reaction is not hysterical but calculated.

In verse three she watches the apothecary at work and is fascinated by what he is doing. She is in no hurry. She takes pleasure in the preparations. This is better than dancing in the king's palace.

DID YOU KNOW?

When Robert Browning published his wife's Sonnets he said that they were 'the finest Sonnets written in any language since Shakespeare'

DID YOU KNOW?

Elizabeth Barrett was an invalid who spent most of her life in her room under the control of her domineering father. Robert Browning and Elizabeth conducted their courtship largely by letter.

CHECK THE NET

The Browning Pages promote all aspects of the life and work of the poet. www. public.asu.edu.

CHECKPOINT 31

Why do you think the exclamation mark appears so frequently in the poem?

CHECKPOINT 32

What is the significance of the word 'ensnared' in line 30?

She asks questions, taking an interest in the coloured liquids and substances. She is keen to learn and appreciates the contrast between their appearance and their effect:

> And yonder soft phial, the exquisite blue,
> Sure to taste sweetly, – is that poison too?   (lines 15–16)

It is clear in verse five that she is consumed by her need for revenge and wishes that all the contents of the laboratory and the apothecary himself were hers, so that she could carry 'pure death' (line 19) where ever she went. The poisons are 'a wild crowd of invisible pleasures!' (line 18) and the prospect of having such power over others excites her. Her rivals may believe that she is a victim, but this will give her absolute control over life and death. Merely by using a pill or lozenge she could kill Pauline in 'just thirty minutes' (line 22) and Elise, about whose attributes she appears particularly jealous, 'should drop dead' (line 24).

She is excited now and eager in verse seven, though initially she is not happy with the colour. She wants it to be attractive so that the victim will take pleasure in taking the poison that will kill her. This is a further indication of her need to have power, so that she will know the true effects, even as the victim admires it.

In verse eight she says that she does not feel that this poison is sufficient. Here we found out a little more information about her rival. Perhaps it is merely jealousy that makes her say she is bigger and that she has 'masculine eyes' (line 32) but the fact remains that she wants her heart to stop beating. Last night she tried to achieve this by staring at her as the lovers whispered together, in the hope that 'she would fall / Shrivelled' (line 36). But of course this poison will be much more effective, 'Yet this does it all!' (line 36). It no longer matters that she is small. The poison will give her absolute power.

She seeks to punish her ex-lover not through his death but through the pain of watching his new love die in agony. He must have her dying face burnt forever into his memory.

There is a madness about the narrator that has slowly been revealed. In verse eleven she must remove her mask so that it will not interfere with her view of the death of her rival. She is prepared to give all her fortune for the drop that will kill.

As the poem ends she is exhilarated. She feels triumphant. Now we are given the image that would have shocked the original readers, which they would have seen as truly debased behaviour and evidence of her insanity. As she hands over her jewels as payment she tells the apothecary, who we assume to be an old man, to kiss her on her mouth.

Perhaps this is an act of revenge on her ex-lover, though more probably it indicates that she has abandoned all moral sense. She will now return to the ball where she will exact her revenge. The repetition of part of line 12, 'dance at the King's', is an indication of her excitement.

DID YOU KNOW?
When you look at this dramatic **monologue** you can imagine it acted out on the stage. Robert Browning did in fact write a number of plays, though without great success.

STYLE

The **rhythm** of the poem, with its positive **rhyme** scheme, is at odds with the calculating horror of the subject matter. Each verse is presented separately as a complete statement, ending in a full stop. There is no doubt, there is no moral speculation. Everything is clear and decided for this woman. It gives the poem a chilling remorselessness.

Robert Browning takes pleasurable things and turns them upside down. A dance at the palace is now an opportunity for murder. The brightly coloured attractive phials contain poison. A drink will kill. Her beautiful ball gown has dust on it that should be brushed off 'lest horror it brings' (line 47). The old apothecary should eat gold. All these details that represent the reversal of the norm, make the narrator happy and she reveals her pleasure in the anticipation of revenge. We do not hear the apothecary speak but we do not need to. Our attention is entirely focused upon the woman.

THEMES

The emotion behind the poem is hatred and in the grip of such hatred an unhappy woman is prepared to murder. We are drawn into her feelings because we hear her speak. It is as if we are there as she speaks to the apothecary, looking on as the poison is prepared.

As in **'My Last Duchess'**, we ask questions about what is happening and this reveals possibilities. Was she in fact ever the lover of this man? Or is it a complete fantasy? Is that why they are laughing at her in verse two? Or are they actually laughing at her at all? Is she suffering from delusions and paranoia?

Links

Story-telling and character

- My Last Duchess
  (Robert Browning)

- The Man He Killed
  (Thomas Hardy)

Personal vision

- Follower
  (Seamus Heaney)

- Catrin
  (Gillian Clarke)

Love

- Sonnet 130
  (William Shakespeare)

ALFRED TENNYSON, 1842 – Ulysses

1 Ulysses, the legendary King of Ithaca, expresses his wish to escape from his responsibilities.

2 He wants to recapture the excitement of his past one last time before he dies.

3 He will leave his throne to his son and set sail into the sunset.

STRUCTURE

The first verse of five lines reveals in one sentence the extent of Ulysses' unhappiness. He is no longer interested in the role he has to play. He is bored, his home has no warmth and he seems to have little affection for his wife. He regards the people he rules as 'a savage race' (line 4) who concern themselves with petty disputes and merely with day-to-day survival.

If the first verse tells us what he has got in Ithaca, then the second verse outlines what he would like to have in its place. His own desires are different from those of his people. Ulysses wants to recapture the past, to recapture the excitement of his youth. This part of his life brought him the extremes of emotion, pleasure and pain (lines 7–9). He became famous 'For always roaming with a hungry heart' (line 12). He was inquisitive, an explorer and a great warrior who fought at Troy. These experiences defined his life and everything else since then has clearly been an anticlimax. He would like to recapture that time, for there is still much that he has not seen. There is an:

> ...untravelled world, whose margin fades
> For ever and for ever when I move.   (lines 20–21)

He believes that he must make the most of the time he has left. He does not want to 'rust unburnished, not to shine in use' (line 23). This is not the time to accept restrictions. In fact Ulysses says that to stay in one place is to believe that all there is to life is breathing (line 24). He knows that he has little left of his own life but that means that each hour is precious, 'saved / From that eternal silence'

DID YOU KNOW?

Tennyson is the only poet ever to be ennobled on the basis of his skill as a writer.

DID YOU KNOW?

Ithaca, the island kingdom of Ulysses, is now thought to have been what we call Cephalonia.

CHECKPOINT 33

What does 'eternal silence' mean in line 27?

DID YOU KNOW?

Troy was an ancient city, probably in present day Turkey, which an army of Greeks besieged for ten years before it fell when the defenders were tricked by the wooden horse. These stories, loosely based upon historical events, formed the basis of many influential legends such as the *Iliad* and the *Odyssey*.

CHECKPOINT 34

What is Ulysses' opinion of his subjects in Ithaca?

DID YOU KNOW?

Achilles was a great warrior and hero of Homer's *Iliad* who was killed when he was shot in the heel by an arrow fired by Paris at the siege of Troy.

(lines 26-7). Although he is old – a 'gray spirit' (line 30) – he wants to learn new things:

> To follow knowledge like a sinking star,
> Beyond the utmost bound of human thought. (lines 31–2)

Ulysses begins the third verse by telling us that he has decided to pass on the responsibility for government to his son Telemachus. He wants the task and has the patience to make a good ruler who will help his subjects and 'through soft degrees / Subdue them to the useful and the good' (lines 37–8). He does not share his father's frustration and restlessness but is 'centred in the sphere / Of common duties' (lines 39–40). Ulysses accepts that he himself has no interest in day to day responsibility: 'He works his work, I mine' (line 43).

The final verse is addressed to his crew, to 'My mariners' (line 45). They have spent much time together and have experienced many things. They may be old but something noble and significant may still be achieved before 'Death closes all' (line 51). They can perhaps relive their youth when they were 'men that strove with gods' (line 53).

When Ulysses now talks about the end of the day, he is of course talking about the end of his life: "Tis not too late to seek a newer world' (line 57). He wants to explore the furthest extremes of the world before it is too late and his purpose is:

> To sail beyond the sunset, and the baths
> Of all the western stars, until I die. (lines 60–61)

They may indeed reach the 'Happy Isles' (line 63) where great heroes like 'Achilles' (line 64) were taken after their deaths. Though they are not as strong as they were, they have a determination to explore and to test themselves one last time.

STYLE

The poem is written as **blank verse** which gives a natural quality to Ulysses' speech and is divided into four verses with distinct themes. The **rhythm** of the poem, created by the uses of **enjambment** and

caesuras is slow and almost hypnotic as befits an old man setting out on one last adventure and disappearing from the everyday world.

THEMES

The poem is an example of how the title can be an integral part of the work. If we know who Ulysses was then we can fill in more of the background. Once we do this, a slightly different picture of the man may emerge.

In the original Greek legends, Ulysses was called Odysseus and the famous poem by Homer, the *Odyssey*, is about his ten-year journey home after the end of the Trojan War. He has many adventures where he is saved by his intelligence and resourcefulness. When he finally arrives home he finds that his wife Penelope has waited for him, confident that he will return.

Some people might now see Ulysses as a man who is attempting to escape from his responsibilities and who repays his wife for her loyalty by returning to a self-indulgent lifestyle of travel and adventure. Do his mariners really want to leave their homes once more? Will they really share his enthusiasm?

If we pursue this interpretation, then Ulysses' stately and measured language becomes rather pompous. This of course is one of the

DID YOU KNOW?
Near the end of his life Tennyson made a recording of himself on wax cylinders reciting his work. So we can still hear his voice today.

DID YOU KNOW?

Tennyson was tall and very strong. He once carried a pony round the table during dinner!

defining qualities of the **dramatic monologue,** that it can support different interpretations as values in society change over time. A Victorian reader may not have accepted this version but a reader hearing Ulysses speak today may well interpret his words in a critical way.

All the excitement that made Ulysses famous happened when he was younger. Now he is living in the shadow of that fame. Nothing that has happened since has ever rivalled the pleasure of those days. He speaks of his desire to recapture his youth before it is too late. He wishes to leave responsibility, to escape the tedium of his life and turn back the clock. He does not want to fulfil his obligations to his wife, his son or his subjects. But he will have to face up to the reality of aging and of death. He will seek and explore before he does indeed meet up with Achilles in death.

Links

Character
- The Last Duchess (Robert Browning)
- The Laboratory (Robert Browning)

Attitude to death
- Tichborne's Elegy (Charles Tichborne)
- On my first Sonne (Ben Jonson)

- Mid-Term Break (Seamus Heaney)
- Cold Knap Lake (Gillian Clarke)

Importance of memory
- Death of a Naturalist (Seamus Heaney)
- Catrin (Gillian Clarke)

Now take a break!

OLIVER GOLDSMITH, 1770 – The Village Schoolmaster

1 This is an extract from a much longer poem called 'The Deserted Village'.

2 Oliver Goldsmith remembers the village schoolmaster and the effect and influence he had upon his pupils and the community as a whole.

3 A once-thriving village is now deserted as the inhabitants have moved away.

4 The poet thinks back to a time when it was busy and full of life.

STRUCTURE

As he walks round the village, Oliver Goldsmith points out the old village school. It was a noisy place but the schoolmaster was 'skilled to rule' (line 3) and was in complete control. Truants knew that they would be dealt with firmly, for he was very strict (line 5). They would try to win favour by laughing loudly at his jokes 'with counterfeited glee' (line 9). He knew lots of jokes and the implication is that he expected his pupils to laugh at them.

Certainly his moods were a vital part of the classroom, affecting everyone else and were thus carefully observed:

> Full well the busy whisper, circling round
> Conveyed the dismal tidings when he frowned; (lines 11–12)

The repetition of the words 'Full well' in lines 9 and 11 links the light hearted moments in the classroom with these more tense occasions.

Oliver Goldsmith, though, excuses him. He was kind and, if he appeared rather too strict, it was only because he believed in the importance of learning (lines 13–14). He was much respected by the small community in which he lived. To them his knowledge seemed incredible, for he had skills that they did not possess in writing and mathematics (lines 15–16). He could calculate 'terms' (line 17) and anticipate the seasons and festivals, a skill that to simple villagers

? DID YOU KNOW?

Although Goldsmith was socially very clumsy and people often laughed at him, the artist Joshua Reynolds said of him, 'Wherever he was there was no yawning'.

CHECKPOINT 35

What impressed the villagers about the schoolmaster's vocabulary?

DID YOU KNOW?

Oliver Goldsmith spent a year touring Europe in 1755. He supported himself by playing the flute.

without calendars appeared remarkable. In fact they really believed he was so clever that he could even calculate the volume of barrels (line 18). They were indeed in awe of his vocabulary and his knowledge:

> And still they gazed, and still the wonder grew
> That one small head could carry all he knew. (lines 23–4)

STYLE

Oliver Goldsmith's **couplets** reflect the status the schoolmaster had. They have positive **rhymes**, each couplet ending in a definitive piece of punctuation that gives the rhymes additional emphasis. The first twelve lines deal with the schoolmaster as he is in school. The second twelve deal with his importance to the whole village.

THEMES

The poem displays the complete respect that the villagers had for the schoolmaster who was a giant in their small community. However, Goldsmith's implied attitude is coloured by a very delicate **irony**. Can you detect where a more critical attitude is implied in the poem?

Oliver Goldsmith gives a picture of the villagers themselves and their simple lives. Isolated villages relied upon individuals who could read, who could predict festivals, even days of the week, and solve disputes. A little knowledge would make them very important people in the village.

Links

Respect

- Digging (Seamus Heaney)
- Cold Knap Lake (Gillian Clarke)

More complex characterisation

- My Last Duchess (Robert Browning)
- The Laboratory (Robert Browning)

ALFRED TENNYSON, 1851 – The Eagle

1 Alfred Tennyson describes an eagle that looks down upon the world.

2 He tries to capture the presence and the power of the eagle in two short verses.

DID YOU KNOW?

Alfred Tennyson is usually referred to as Alfred, Lord Tennyson after he was made a baron in 1884.

STRUCTURE

The bird 'clasps the crag' (line 1) as if he owns it. He stands there in splendid isolation. He is close to the sun, much closer than man can ever be, surrounded by the blue of the sky (line 3). This is his world, not the world of man.

The eagle can look down upon the sea below him. It is so far beneath him that it seems 'wrinkled' and it 'crawls' (line 4), a word that strips the ocean of its majesty. Real power lies with the eagle who, when he chooses, can fall from the 'mountain walls' (line 5) where he sits 'like a thunderbolt' (line 6). This **simile** emphasises the huge power that the bird possesses.

CHECK THE NET

The Victorian Web has a great deal of very useful information on the Victorian age, including pages on Gerard Manley Hopkins, Alfred Tennyson and Robert Browning:
www.65.107.211. 206/Victorian.

CHECKPOINT 36

Which part of the eagle does Tennyson **not** refer to directly in the first line but which is implied?

STYLE

The first line is dominated by hard 'c' sounds – 'clasps', 'crags' and 'crooked'. These words immediately establish the nature of the bird as fierce, domineering and in control.

Tennyson here is particularly interested in capturing the eagle's power and its haughty superiority perched in the mountains.

THEMES

There is no doubt about the bird's gender. It is reinforced in every line except line two. Perhaps something of the Victorian male's sense of his own power and superiority is reflected by this depiction.

Yet in this poem, animals inhabit a different world which man cannot access. We can watch the eagle in the sky but we can never experience its world.

Links

Animals

- Perch
  (Seamus Heaney)
- The Eagle
  (Alfred Tennyson)

Animals and the human world

- The Field-Mouse
  (Gillian Clarke)
- A Difficult Birth
  (Gillian Clarke)

GERARD MANLEY HOPKINS, 1881 – Inversnaid

DID YOU KNOW?

Inversnaid is on the north-eastern shore of Loch Lomond in the west of Scotland.

❶ **Gerard Manley Hopkins describes the experience of watching a mountain stream turn into a waterfall.**

STRUCTURE

'Inversnaid' has a simple inspiration. What Gerard Manley Hopkins attempts is to use words to describe the complete experience of watching the stream and a waterfall. By compressing words together he is able to give a much more intense impression. We can see this immediately in the first two lines. The stream ('burn') is 'horseback brown'. This suggests the colour of the water and also the speed of its movement. It roars down, the word 'rollrock' (line 2) describing its power. It creates foam (line 3) that looks like wool on the water.

This foam is caught by a 'windpuff' (line 5) as the water falls into a pool and circles around. The pool where it enters is so dark that it appears to have the power to wipe away all emotion (line 8). This darkness could be a symbol of despair, perhaps a symbol of life disappearing. But the water has such force that it drowns out such human feelings.

Gerard Manley Hopkins then moves on in verse three to describe the land on either side of the stream. It is wild untended moorland with 'Wiry heathpacks' (line 11). Such wild places, untouched by mankind, should be preserved because they speak of the power of the natural world:

> What would the world be, once bereft
> Of wet and of wildness? Let them be left, (lines 13–14)

STYLE

This is a very musical poem, held together by its regular rhyme scheme and by the use of consonants. This is called assonance. In the first verse, for example, the dominant sounds are 'b' 'r' and 'f'. As verse two moves into verse three the sound turns to 'd' and in the final verse the 'w' sound dominates.

This musicality gives the poem its power and rhythm. It flows, with the hard sounds suggesting the way the water rushes and splashes and slaps on the rocks. These are things associated with a fast-moving stream. Gerard Manley Hopkins is attempting to make you feel as if you are there watching the waterfall drop down into a pool. He compresses its energy into carefully chosen words. The dark water is like a powerful horse rocking at speed down a road.

 CHECK THE NET

This Gerard Manley Hopkins website has lots of material about the poet: **www. creighton. edu/~dcallon/ Hopkins**.

CHECKPOINT 37

The waterfall that Gerard Manley Hopkins writes about is called The Mare's Tail. How do you think this could have influenced the making of the poem?

 DID YOU KNOW?

'Sprung Rhythm' was an attempt by Gerard Manley Hopkins to introduce a new rhythm to the structure of poetry, which he hoped would bring it closer to common speech.

DID YOU KNOW?

The poem was written on 28 September 1881.

DID YOU KNOW?

After a break from writing poetry (see **Setting and background)**, Gerard Manley Hopkins was inspired to start writing poetry again by the sinking of a ship called *The Deutschland* at the mouth of the river Thames in 1875, in which five nuns were drowned. He offered the poem to the Jesuit journal *The Month* but the editor said that he dared not publish it!

The water has the power to move rocks. All this is suggested in the first ten words of the poem.

In the second verse there is a clear progression in emotions. We start with 'frowning' (line 7) which leads to 'Despair' (line 8) which leads perhaps to suicide – 'drowning' (line 8) – in the hypnotic circling of the water. These words reflect Gerard Manley Hopkins' feelings at this time. However the power of the water wipes away all such human uncertainty.

The plea in the last verse, that such places should remain untouched, is emphasised by the repetition of key words.

THEMES

Gerard Manley Hopkins' relationship with nature marks this out as an important poem. He displays unquestioning admiration for nature and attempts to create a complete picture of a natural phenomenon.

In '**Inversnaid**' there is no human influence. That is part of its attraction to the poet. Here he can escape from the pressures and tensions of his life and lose himself in the power of nature.

Links

Nature

- Perch (Seamus Heaney)
- The Eagle (Alfred Tennyson)
- Patrolling Barnegat (Walt Whitman)

Nature and the human world

- Gillian Clarke's poems – A Difficult Birth, The Field-Mouse, etc.

Untroubled by the human world

- Sonnet (John Clare)

JOHN CLARE, 1841 – Sonnet

1 John Clare reveals his admiration for nature.

2 He identifies the things that he likes to see.

STRUCTURE

John Clare tells us about the things in nature that he enjoys. It is above all else a personal statement of an uncomplicated relationship with nature. He tells us of the things he sees that give him pleasure.

He enjoys the summer brightness and the white clouds in the sky. He then moves the focus of his attention to the details before him, the wild flowers, the water lilies and the creatures that move through the picture he sees. He describes an idyllic scene, with rustling reeds and nesting moorhens. The willow hanging over the 'clear deep lake' (line 10) has a perfect shape.

John Clare provides us with a vivid description. It is not, though, a static one. It has in it a sense of movement as if the poem is powered by the summer breeze. The white clouds are 'sailing to the north' (line 2), the moorhen's nest is 'floating' (line 8), the 'flower head swings' (line 11). The insects are flying on 'happy wings' (line 12) and the beetles seem to be playing in the 'clear lake' (line 14). Nature is at ease with itself, happy and untroubled. The words he chooses are gentle ones. There is nothing abrupt or aggressive. Everything is calm and measured. The water is pure and there is no intrusion from human beings. The fact that man is excluded from the picture is significant, as if there is nothing he can contribute to the beauty of the scene.

STYLE

The **sonnet** has a simple pattern, the traditional fourteen lines, here presented as seven **couplets**. It has a regularity and a shape. The lack of punctuation ensures that the poem maintains a rhythm that places emphasis upon the rhymed words. The words 'I love' are repeated three times along with 'I like'. This helps to tie the piece

DID YOU KNOW?

At the time this poem was written Clare's mental instability was becoming established; perhaps we can see in it a yearning for healing, peace and simplicity.

CHECKPOINT 38

What words are used at the start of some of the lines that indicate that this poem is a very personal picture?

together and states clearly the feelings that have inspired John Clare to write. Such simplicity is a feature of his work and makes his poetry very accessible.

THEMES

The poem has an innocence at its heart. Nature is attractive and balanced with no need of humankind. It is something that exists to make the poet feel better. He enjoys looking at it as if it were a painting. In this way it provides an important contrast with the work of other poets in this selection.

Gerard Manley Hopkins tries to give us the complete experience of a wild and untamed landscape. John Clare, however, describes what he sees in an uncomplicated way. There is clearly a difference in the scenes that are presented, with the wilderness of Inversnaid emphasised by the power of the water that contrasts with the gentle pastoral scene and the tranquil clear lake that Clare can see. In both cases, though, nature persists without the need for mankind.

When we realise that this poem was written when his mental instability was becoming established, perhaps we can then see in it a yearning for healing peace and simplicity. Mankind perhaps cannot improve upon what the poet sees, but only contributes confusion and disharmony to such a timeless picture.

Links

Nature

- Inversnaid
  (Gerard Manley Hopkins)

- Perch
  (Seamus Heaney)

- The Eagle
  (Alfred Tennyson)

- Patrolling Barnegat
  (Walt Whitman)

Human involvement

- The Field-Mouse
  (Gillian Clarke)

- Death of a Naturalist
  (Seamus Heaney)

Now take a break!

FROM WHICH POEM?

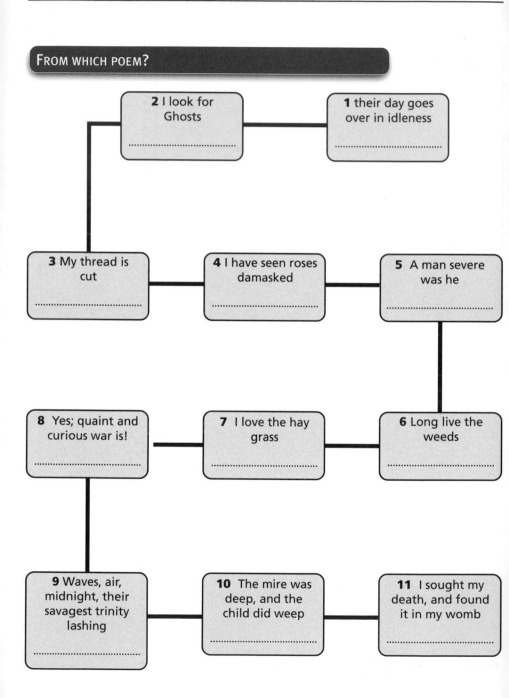

2 I look for Ghosts

....

1 their day goes over in idleness

....

3 My thread is cut

....

4 I have seen roses damasked

....

5 A man severe was he

....

8 Yes; quaint and curious war is!

....

7 I love the hay grass

....

6 Long live the weeds

....

9 Waves, air, midnight, their savagest trinity lashing

....

10 The mire was deep, and the child did weep

....

11 I sought my death, and found it in my womb

....

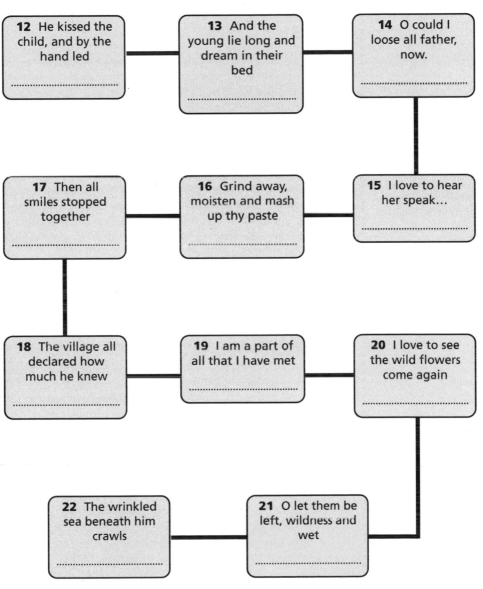

12 He kissed the child, and by the hand led
....

13 And the young lie long and dream in their bed
....

14 O could I loose all father, now.
....

15 I love to hear her speak...
....

16 Grind away, moisten and mash up thy paste
....

17 Then all smiles stopped together
....

18 The village all declared how much he knew
....

19 I am a part of all that I have met
....

20 I love to see the wild flowers come again
....

21 O let them be left, wildness and wet
....

22 The wrinkled sea beneath him crawls
....

Check your answers on p. 140.

PART THREE

COMMENTARY

THEMES

In this section we will be looking at ideas, feelings and attitudes. There are significant overlaps between these three areas. An attitude towards something can create a feeling about an issue that can quickly become an idea. Such divisions are not always natural but they may well help you bring this wide-ranging selection of poetry together in your mind.

EXAMINER'S SECRET

Learn how to spell **simile**. Like you it has only got two 'i's.

There are lots of ideas here that run between the poems and bring them together and not all the possibilities can be explored in this section. You must keep your mind open to possibilities and explore any that occur to you. What you are then looking for is evidence so that you can either compare or contrast the writers' states of mind or techniques.

This is an important point. You can bring your own thoughts and insights to the study of poetry. But you must be able to support what you say with examples from the text.

All the poems in this Anthology have their own merits and they all speak to us. Just because they are not mentioned frequently it should not be taken as a suggestion that they have less merit or relevance. All have important and interesting things to say. You need to become familiar with all the poems and listen to what they tell us. You certainly won't regret it.

Just think of how remarkable it is that we can have access not only to someone else's thoughts and feelings but also to the thoughts and feelings of someone who lived a long time ago. What we see is that the things that drive poets have not changed much. Social conditions might have altered but poets are driven to write about the big issues – love, life, death, about what it actually all might mean. In this way poetry, like all great writing, establishes connections across the centuries. Pre-1914, Post-1914, it doesn't matter. What is important is what the poet has to say to us.

IDEAS

1. Nature

Key poems	
Seamus Heaney	Storm on the Island
Seamus Heaney	Perch
Seamus Heaney	Blackberry-Picking
Seamus Heaney	Death of a Naturalist
Gillian Clarke	A Difficult Birth
Gillian Clarke	The Field-Mouse
Walt Whitman	Patrolling Barnegat
Gerard Manley Hopkins	Inversnaid
John Clare	Sonnet

The idea of nature runs through much of this selection. It is something to which the poets themselves are drawn and to which they respond in different ways. On the one hand you have John Clare in 'Sonnet' who sees the natural world as a sanctuary, a place of tranquillity and harmony. There is gentle movement and a sense of innocent pleasure. This reflects the sort of naturalist that Seamus Heaney was as a child. It is the way many see nature and the reason why they are drawn to it. Seamus Heaney collected tadpoles and enjoyed watching them develop. Nature was contained and predictable. But nature is not like this. What happens to Seamus Heaney in 'Death of a Naturalist' is that he has to confront the truth – that frogs have sex. They are no longer clever creatures that can change colour. They are 'gross-bellied...their loose necks pulsed like snails' (lines 27–8). Such reality kills his innocent interest in nature. He can still observe nature as he does in 'Perch' but he can never see it with child-like simplicity again. Nature is something that is completely indifferent to man. It is a world that we can observe but never access.

Gerard Manley Hopkins in **'Inversnaid'** observes nature and describes it as John Clare does but he wants to do more that just paint a picture. He creates new word combinations to try to replicate the experience of what he saw. There are no people in what he describes. He does not need them. He wants to show the grandeur of nature against which human concerns seem unimportant: 'It rounds and rounds Despair to drowning' (line 8). It has a strength and power that goes far beyond human capability. The power of nature is evident in **'Patrolling Barnegat'** by Walt Whitman where the pounding of the rhyme parallels the pounding of the sea. We can see that these poets do not just want to describe nature, they want the reader to experience it, to feel its power and to realise that in comparison, man is often small and insignificant. We cannot influence it at all. All humans can do is to watch and to take shelter. Look at Seamus Heaney's **'Storm on the Island'** in which people burrow into the ground to escape the consequences of the wind. This stresses the importance of three essential elements. The earth, the water and the air feature strongly in his work.

Clarke's verse is firmly rooted in a close observation of the natural world but she uses what she sees to different effect. This can be seen particularly in **'A Difficult Birth'** where her experiences lead to a detailed understanding of the ewe's labour. But what we also see is how Clarke can link the natural world with other events, drawing comparisons between them. The link between the peace process in Northern Ireland and the delivery of the lambs is made clear. Both are uncertain and dangerous processes but they have within them the possibility for hope and resurrection. In **'The Field-Mouse'** she moves from the consequences of harvesting to the suffering in conflict in Central Europe. Not only does it involve the mouse as a symbol of suffering and vulnerability, but she also draws in powerful references to the suffering of children. For Clarke, nature is a metaphor that can shed light upon events in human affairs.

EXAMINER'S SECRET

Ask yourself: How does the writer achieve their effects?

This sort of threat or sadness does not appear in John Clare's **'Sonnet'**. But for the other poets here the natural world is not a picture. It can be powerful like the eagle that Alfred Tennyson describes and, as Seamus Heaney shows us, it can be messy, untidy and threatening. The flax-dam challenges simple ideas about nature.

? DID YOU KNOW?
Gillian Clarke says 'Understanding the poem is down to you. You don't need me or your teacher, or a book, to tell you how to respond to it'

In Heaney's poem **'Blackberry-Picking'** there is no simple vision either. There may be a glut of fruit that must be collected, but it contains the elements of its own destruction leading to inevitable disappointment.

2 The Seasons

> **Key poems**
>
> | | |
> |---|---|
> | Seamus Heaney | Blackberry-Picking |
> | Seamus Heaney | At a Potato Digging |
> | Gillian Clarke | Mali |
> | Gillian Clarke | A Difficult Birth |
> | Gillian Clarke | The Field-Mouse |
> | Gillian Clarke | October |
> | Gillian Clarke | On the Train |
> | Gerard Manley Hopkins | Inversnaid |

The poets are aware that events have their own appropriate time, that things happen to a natural rhythm when they are supposed to happen, as part of an annual cycle. Spring is the time for birth, for

EXAMINER'S SECRET
Look after your Anthology. It is not on sale in bookshops. It is only available from the Examination Board.

lambing. Thus we have **'A Difficult Birth'** which connects the annual event of lambing and introduces Christian imagery, linking the positive elements of the Easter story with the chance for peace in Northern Ireland.

In John Clare's **'Sonnet'** there is a description of the height of summer, a time of peace and warmth. Life is easy, unthreatening and serene. There is a direct contrast with Gillian Clarke's vision of summer in **'The Field-Mouse'**. Here summer is much more threatening and ominous. There is death and destruction (a mouse killed, flowers destroyed) and there is bad news on the radio, 'the air hums with jets' (line 2).

Late summer is the time for blackberries. Collecting them is an annual event. In his poem **'Blackberry-Picking'** Seamus Heaney describes how he went to pick them even though he knew that they would inevitably rot, with their destruction by a 'rat-grey fungus' (line 19). It is also the time when Gillian Clarke's granddaughter Mali was born. In her poem **'Mali'** we are made aware of how human affairs connect with the phases of the moon, how our feelings can match the 'unmistakable brim and tug of the tide' (line 2).

As summer moves into autumn the rivers and streams are swollen as we see in **'Inversnaid'**. This can lead to the flooding through which Clarke travels in **'On the Train'**. In October as the weather changes, as the wind shakes the trees and the plants reach the end of their natural cycle, so there is death in the human world too. The weather matches the mood of Gillian Clarke's poem **'October'** as her friend is buried. She is particularly sensitive to the times of the year and like the other poets here she attaches certain feelings to the different seasons. Heaney looks instead at annual events like harvesting the potatoes and collecting the blackberries and the feelings that return every year as they do so.

It is in this way that the place of humankind is confirmed. We are part of the natural world, not separated from it. As the seasons unfold, so does life, moving inevitably from birth to death, our final destination.

3. The Generations

> ### Key poems
>
> | | |
> |---|---|
> | Seamus Heaney | **Digging** |
> | Seamus Heaney | **Follower** |
> | Gillian Clarke | **Catrin** |
> | Gillian Clarke | **Mali** |
> | Alfred Tennyson | **Ulysses** |
> | W. B. Yeats | **The Song of the Old Mother** |
> | William Wordsworth | **The Affliction of Margaret** |

The relationship between the generations within a family forms a major part of these poems. As a theme it does come close to Childhood (see **Theme on Childhood**), but there are sufficient differences to make them stand apart. The important word in this thematic idea is *responsibility*.

It is the sense of responsibility that drives the old woman in Yeats' poem to get up every morning to carry on with her duties for an ungrateful family. This must be exhausting and Ulysses takes up this theme in Alfred Tennyson's poem. He no longer wants to accept the responsibility that comes with sovereignty. He is ready to abdicate from that and pass the responsibility on to his son Telemachus who, he says, is more suited to this sort of thing anyway. Ulysses sees himself as a free spirit that should not be contained. He believes that his own personal ambitions are more important than his duty. He wants to leave his responsibility and his son behind.

An unbreakable bond, however, exists within other families. William Wordsworth displays this in 'The Affliction of Margaret'. Margaret's affliction is a lack of news about her son. She wants information at a time when communication was not so easy as it is today. She has heard nothing for seven years from her son who she describes as 'an object beauteous to behold' (line 16). Now sadness and anxiety consume her. The strength of the maternal feeling so

CHECK THE NET

If you need to check on any of the details of the examination syllabus, then visit **www.aqa.org.uk**.

EXAMINER'S SECRET

To get the higher marks don't just tell the story.

clearly presented links with the work and the priorities of Gillian Clarke. The importance of family and the bloodline that binds is at the heart of **'Mali'**. This is represented graphically in **'Catrin'** by the image of the rope that connects mother and daughter together, initially physically and then **metaphorically**

In Seamus Heaney's poetry the different generations within a family are examined. There are significant differences between them as we see in **'Digging'**. The poet can never hope to rival the family's skill in apparently simple tasks. He respects their abilities to provide for the family. Perhaps he feels guilty that he cannot do so in the same way. He will break that family tradition and 'dig' (line 31) with his pen.

This sense of respect is central to his relationship with his father. Now that he is an adult, Seamus Heaney has to be prepared to accept his responsibilities as a consequence of family ties based on respect and love. This is presented in **'Follower'** and its title is significant because it refers to both father and son. When he was a child Seamus Heaney was the follower. He followed his father, trying to emulate him. Now their roles have been reversed. Now it is his father who stumbles. Where he had once been a nuisance, perhaps he finds his father a nuisance now. The responsibility is there and 'will not go away' (line 24).

FEELINGS

1 Fear and dread

Key poems

Seamus Heaney	Storm on the Island
Seamus Heaney	At a Potato Digging
Gillian Clarke	The Field-Mouse
Gillian Clarke	On the Train
William Wordsworth	The Affliction of Margaret
Charles Tichborne	Elegy
Walt Whitman	Patrolling Barnegat

Such feelings as fear and dread can make poems particularly powerful. Writers can establish feelings through their choice of images and words that create the atmosphere and the mood, which in turn affects the way a reader responds.

Look for example at Clarke's **'On the Train'** as she travels and looks out of the window and sees flooded fields. This is an accurate detail, for there was a particularly wet October that year. But the use of the word 'flooded' (line 1) creates a sense of foreboding. Then in the next verse she describes the doomed train full of unsuspecting passengers as a 'blazing bone ship' (line 12). This is a chilling image that makes a significant contribution to the creation of mood. There is a similar sense of apprehension created in **'The Field-Mouse'**. Here she uses the news on the radio, the jet plane, and the killed flowers in the first ten lines to set the context of the poem.

The context of Charles Tichborne's **'Elegy'** is exacerbated by the negative words with which he ends his lines and creates a sense of misery and dread. There is a real sense of anxiety in **'The Affliction of Margaret'** by William Wordsworth where she worries about what has happened to her son:

EXAMINER'S SECRET

Make sure you comment on the particular element that the examiner asks for in the question. Don't write generally, keep focused.

> My apprehensions come in crowds;
> I dread the rustling of the grass;   (lines 64–5)

We are shown Margaret's fears because she speaks to us directly. It is as if she is addressing us personally so that we can hear and feel her fears.

'**At a Potato Digging**' by Seamus Heaney is based entirely upon the sense of dread that consumes the workers in the fields who every year have to confront the possibility that the earth that sustains them will turn against them. The effects of the famine can never be forgotten. The trust that once existed between the workers and the earth has been destroyed. The blight could return at any time and turn their harvest into 'skulls' (line 30). There is certainly fear in confronting the power of nature. Seamus Heaney is faced with the vast impersonal power of the wind in '**Storm on the Island**'. The imagery he chooses emphasises the threat that the wind poses. People hide away from it in fear and appear to be under attack. The wind 'dives' (line 16) 'strafes invisibly' (line 17) and yet is everywhere at the same time: 'It is a huge nothing that we fear' (line 19).

EXAMINER'S SECRET

Make sure you can spell 'Seamus' and 'Heaney'. There is nothing quite so off-putting for a marker than to see the writer's name spelt incorrectly.

'**Patrolling Barnegat**' has a similar sense of dread. The storm attacks man with 'demoniac laughter' (line 3). Here the fear is

created by the vocabulary and the relentless sound of the storm that
rolls all through the poem.

2 Disappointment

DID YOU
KNOW?
On her web site
Gillian Clarke urges
readers not to be
frightened of
poetry: 'It is in
English and the
poet's a human
being like you'.

Key poems

Seamus Heaney	**Blackberry-Picking**
Gillian Clarke	**Cold Knap Lake**
Charles Tichborne	**Elegy**
Robert Browning	**My Last Duchess**
Alfred Tennyson	**Ulysses**

Disappointment is an inevitable part of life, something that we must
all come to terms with to a greater or lesser degree. This theme of
sadness is clear in a range of these poems.

Perhaps disappointment is not a strong enough word to encapsulate
Charles Tichborne's feelings as he prepares for death. All his hopes
and ambitions now seem worthless as he contemplates horrific
execution. It all seems to have been a waste of time.

At a simple level there is the disappointment that the Duke of Ferrara
experiences in his previous duchess in Robert Browning's poem. He
is disappointed that she did not seem to know what was expected of
her. In this poem his disappointment is expressed in his speech to the
envoy. We can hear what he says, as well as recognise the way he says
it with an apparent level of exasperation, pretending to choose the
right words to describe behaviour that he cannot understand.

In Seamus Heaney's **'Blackberry-Picking'** disappointment lies at
the very centre of the poem and is expressed through the **image** of
the fruits themselves and what they represent. Every year the poet is
driven to collect them. He has an instinctive urge to gather and
hoard. And every year they rot. His hopes are doomed to
disappointment because when he collects the blackberries he also
unwittingly collects the thing that will destroy them.

There is also a sense of disappointment present in **'Cold Knap Lake'** by Gillian Clarke. Memories can be lost and life cannot always be breathed into them. The beautiful swans always take off and fly away, leaving the lake behind with just the 'satiny mud' (line 18). As a result she cannot access all the things in her past that have made her what she is.

Ulysses in Alfred Tennyson's poem looks back in old age with disappointment at the way his life has turned out. After all the excitement and success of his youth when he became 'a name / For always roaming with a hungry heart' (lines 11–12), now he feels trapped 'among these barren crags' (line 2). He has to break free and at least we feel that he has the courage to confront and to change things, even if it does mean that he is turning his back upon his responsibilities.

3 Admiration

**EXAMINER'S
SECRET**

Don't forget to
show admiration for
the poets!

Key poems	
Seamus Heaney	Digging
Seamus Heaney	Follower
Gillian Clarke	Cold Knap Lake
Oliver Goldsmith	The Village Schoolmaster
William Shakespeare	Sonnet 130

Admiration is expressed in many different ways in these poems. William Shakespeare in **'Sonnet 130'** expresses his love and admiration for the woman who has come to be known as 'The Dark Lady' by stripping away all sense of the artificial. He does not need to use false comparisons because he admires her for what she is – a real woman – and he wants her to realise this. This is a very flattering thing for him to say because it shows that he connects with her reality rather than with artificiality.

In Seamus Heaney's **'Digging'** and **'Follower'** there is a real sense of admiration of the skill displayed by his father, skill that he will never acquire. Both the poet's father and grandfather were simple men leading an unsophisticated life but they were highly accomplished at the things that were important to maintain their families by providing food and warmth. Digging in particular may appear a simple task but they displayed precision and skill.

Ulysses in Alfred Tennyson's poem shows admiration for his son Telemachus who displays talents in areas that he himself is about to reject. He is more interested in pursuing his own ambitions but he is comfortable with the idea of passing on the kingdom of Ithaca to his son.

Oliver Goldsmith's poem **'The Village Schoolmaster'** is an extended impression of a man much admired in his small village. He has numerous skills that make him a celebrity. His opinions and his expert knowledge are sought and the villagers marvel at all the things he knows. Perhaps he does enjoy his status in the village amongst people who are much simpler than him. Nevertheless the Schoolmaster is comfortable with the role he has to play. There is a contrast here with Ulysses who does not enjoy the company of the people in his kingdom. The schoolmaster likes the attention and the respect that he receives.

Gillian Clarke admires the way her mother saved a child's life in **'Cold Knap Lake'**: 'my mother gave a stranger's child her breath' (line 8). This is a gift of life that characterises women for Clarke. She admires mothers who give life and support. In **'Baby-sitting'** she speaks of the impossibility of relating to someone else's child in the same way as you relate to your own but here her mother brings a child back from the dead. The men who appear in her poems are rarely described in such admiring terms.

EXAMINER'S SECRET
Don't waste time writing out the question at the start of your answer. The examiner already knows what it is.

EXAMINER'S SECRET
The examiners are more interested in what you have to say about the poem than what you know about the poet.

EXAMINER'S SECRET
As part of your planning for your answer underline key words in the title, like the topic and the selected poems.

ATTITUDES

1 Attitudes towards death

Key poems

Seamus Heaney	Mid-Term Break
Gillian Clarke	October
Gillian Clarke	The Field-Mouse
Ben Jonson	On my First Sonne
Charles Tichborne	Elegy
Thomas Hardy	The Man He Killed
Robert Browning	My Last Duchess
Robert Browning	The Laboratory
Alfred Tennyson	Ulysses

Death is a striking theme that runs through these poems and towards which the poets have different attitudes. It is part of all our lives and we have to find our own way of dealing with it. The poets here are no different from the rest of us.

Of course Charles Tichborne's 'Elegy' stands out here because of the way he has to accept and prepare for his own imminent death. It makes him consider his life and how little he now feels he has achieved. He can feel his death rushing towards him and he knows that he can do nothing about it. This contrasts with the casual attitude to the death of his wife that the Duke of Ferrara displays in 'My Last Duchess'. She was young and lively but ultimately disposable. Her murder is seen as justifiable and inevitable, the action of a completely reasonable but exasperated man. What is striking, though, is Robert Browning's skill in the poem, for it still communicates to the reader the horror of what he has arranged.

In 'The Laboratory' the narrator regards death as her right. She experiences no doubts or any sort of moral crisis in planning death. She can exact her revenge and looks forward to the suffering she can cause. She is excited at the prospect of the ultimate control that the poison will give her – the power to decide who will live and who will die. For such control she will sacrifice all her wealth. She is a woman consumed by the need for revenge.

Death in Thomas Hardy's poem **'The Man He Killed'** is part of a soldier's obligations. It is why he exists. If he had not killed the other man then he would have killed him. Death is thus justified, even expected, but the narrator is puzzled by the reversal that takes place in normal social behaviour.

In Ben Jonson's poem **'On my first Sonne'** death is seen to be much crueller because the death takes away the 'child of my right hand' (line 1). His son will be frozen in time. He will never change or develop. What he was is what he will always be. He tries to find consolation by remembering that his son has escaped pain and disappointment and old age. It is hard, though, to bid farewell to his son. A similar feeling for the tragic loss of a young and incomplete life is presented to us in Seamus Heaney's **'Mid-Term Break'**. This poem is particularly affecting because of the simplicity of the language that is used. We see the event through Heaney's young eyes without judgement. It is as if the poet was confused by what happened, almost numb. The strength of his poem lies in the fact we can see it all for ourselves.

The death of the mouse, and by association the death of children in conflict, gives **'The Field-Mouse'** by Gillian Clarke much of its power. Here Gillian Clarke links the death of a single mouse with much wider issues. Perhaps we prefer to grieve for an injured mouse since it is less painful than grieving for the destruction of a nation.

In Clarke's poem **'October'** the death of a friend acts as a creative spur for the writer. She becomes aware that it will indeed happen to her one day and she feels the need to hold back time in order to achieve what she would like. Ulysses, however, seems to welcome death and is ready to sail off into a sunset from which he will never return. His exciting past means that he is unwilling to accept an ordinary future.

EXAMINER'S SECRET

Don't be afraid to show enthusiasm. If you are writing about one of the poems that you really like then say so. It shows that you have engaged with what you read.

2. Attitudes towards childhood

> **Key poems**
>
> | | |
> |---|---|
> | Seamus Heaney | Blackberry-Picking |
> | Seamus Heaney | Death of a Naturalist |
> | Gillian Clarke | Catrin |
> | Gillian Clarke | Baby-sitting |
> | Gillian Clarke | Mali |
> | Gillian Clarke | The Field-Mouse |
> | William Wordsworth | The Affliction of Margaret |

Children are the next generation. They are the means by which the species will move forward. Humans have an instinctive need to protect them and do so over a period of time that is longer than that for most other animals. The bonds particularly between parents and children are powerful and are explored by a number of poems here. In her poem **'Catrin'** Gillian Clarke provides the perfect metaphor for this bond, the rope that binds a mother to her children. This is further emphasised in **'Baby-sitting'** where that bond does not exist. Her attitude to the child is one of duty. She is baby-sitting and will do what she has to do. But she is not the mother, and the child knows that too. With her own children, with her granddaughter in **'Mali'** she is 'hooked again, life-sentenced' (line 20) – an image that encapsulates her sense that such feelings are instinctive and inescapable. Her instinctive desire to protect children can be seen in **'The Field-Mouse'** but she also knows that at the same time elsewhere they are made vulnerable and are in danger.

The social context may have changed but this fundamental human experience transcends time and culture. We can see Clarke's 'rope' in **'The Affliction of Margaret'** by William Wordsworth. Her life has now been consumed by anxiety. If she lives her life through her only child and that child has gone, then she has no life. She now lives with uncertainty. She will forgive him whatever has happened. All she wants is his safe return: 'I wait for day and night / With love and longings infinite' (lines 62–3).

EXAMINER'S SECRET

Plan your approach to the examination carefully. Divide up the available time, allocate a time to each answer and stick to it. In this way you are sure to finish the paper.

Seamus Heaney sees childhood as a time of temporary innocence and enthusiasm that is soon destroyed by experience. He collected tadpoles, just as he collected blackberries but the real world can intrude into childhood and nothing can be the same again. Even children have to come to terms with disappointment, disease and death.

METHODS

IMAGERY

Key poems	
Seamus Heaney	At a Potato Digging
Gillian Clarke	Catrin
Gillian Clarke	A Difficult Birth
Gillian Clarke	The Field-Mouse
W. B. Yeats	The Song of the Old Mother
Alfred Tennyson	Ulysses

Imagery is one of the things that defines poetry. By setting up unusual comparisons or by connecting unexpected ideas, the skilled poets we read in this Anthology can make us see the world differently. When they are well chosen, images add considerably to our understanding. A very effective example of this is in Seamus Heaney's 'At a Potato Digging'. The poet compares potatoes to stones and in doing so compresses a great number of connections and meanings. He then uses the eyes of a potato to move on to their sightlessness and this connects with their hardness to suggest skulls, which in turn becomes an image of death in a famine. Poetry can have such a personal and profound effect because of the uniqueness of the pictures and connections it creates.

In 'Ulysses' Alfred Tennyson uses the highly appropriate image of the galley upon which Ulysses will sail into the setting sun. This image represents death, an old man and his crew setting off on one last adventure. This image adds to the mood created by his stately and measured speech of farewell to his unsatisfying life.

In 'The Song of the Old Mother' the old woman, her life full of work and responsibility, must revive the fire every morning. But as we see at the end of W. B. Yeats' poem, the fire is getting feeble and cold. This is a **metaphor** for the old woman. One day the fire will go out. She will die like the fire. It is a well-chosen image that reflects the old woman perfectly. She is still giving warmth and support. But one day when she no longer has the strength, that will stop.

This is how imagery works. It draws together a fire and an old woman to add another level to our understanding. Another powerful single image is that used by Gillian Clarke in 'Catrin' where the idea of the rope perfectly captures the nature of a child's relationship with a parent. She has other carefully chosen images in her work. In 'The Field-Mouse' the image of the animals as refugees in the context of the collapse of Yugoslavia is powerful and appropriate. The image of the stone rolling away at the end of 'A Difficult Birth' uses the Easter story and the resurrection – or rebirth – of Christ to link to the unexpected delivery of a second lamb and to the sense of hope that comes with the peace process in Northern Ireland.

EXAMINER'S SECRET

If you revise sensibly then there should be no need to stay awake working into the small hours the night before an exam. It is better to have a good night's sleep and so feel refreshed for the exam.

CHARACTERS

<table>
<tr><td colspan="2">Key poems</td></tr>
<tr><td>Seamus Heaney</td><td>Follower</td></tr>
<tr><td>Gillian Clarke</td><td>Catrin</td></tr>
<tr><td>Thomas Hardy</td><td>The Man He Killed</td></tr>
<tr><td>Robert Browning</td><td>My Last Duchess</td></tr>
<tr><td>Alfred Tennyson</td><td>Ulysses</td></tr>
<tr><td>Oliver Goldsmith</td><td>The Village Schoolmaster</td></tr>
</table>

All of us find other people interesting. The things other people do and the things that they say underpin all of our lives. Poets create characters just as novelists do but in different ways. Some poets here write without introducing humans at all and we can see in John Clare, Gerard Manley Hopkins and in Alfred Tennyson's '**The Eagle**' that their desire to express the grandeur and power of nature means that people are not important to them. They wish to explore the timelessness of nature that is not dependent upon people.

Others, however, create characters. They are sometimes created in a description of their actions. This is clear in Gillian Clarke's '**Catrin**' and in Seamus Heaney's '**Follower**'. The former stands there defiantly, the latter is described as a patient man who takes his son with him and carries him on his shoulder. His skill as a farmer is described and adds to our picture.

The character of the schoolmaster in Oliver Goldsmith's poem is presented to us in the things that he does and also in the reactions of others to him. The poet, through his humorous and affectionate picture, establishes the part he plays in the village community. The villagers are tremendously impressed by him because their own lives are perhaps narrow and limited. His knowledge appears almost magical to them. We form the impression that he enjoys their attentions.

EXAMINER'S SECRET
Have a good breakfast on the morning of your examination. You can't perform at your best if you are hungry.

**EXAMINER'S SECRET**
Drink plenty of water when you are revising. It will help your brain to function properly.

Other poets allow their characters to speak and, in doing so, allow them to reveal something of themselves. We see for example that Ulysses seems rather pompous and self-centred. We see the brutality of the Duke of Ferrara in 'My Last Duchess'. In Thomas Hardy's poem 'The Man He Killed' we can see how skilfully he presents the genuine puzzlement of a west-country soldier forced to kill someone he has never met. He is an ordinary man caught up in extra-ordinary events, a genuine sociable sort of man who would buy someone a drink and share a good time with them. It is this that makes this one of the great anti-war poems, because we hear an ordinary man speaking in a simple way.

USE OF FIRST PERSON

Key poems

Seamus Heaney	Mid-Term Break
Gillian Clarke	A Difficult Birth
Robert Browning	My Last Duchess
John Clare	Sonnet

One of the defining elements in poetry is the use of the word 'I'. This indicates just how personal a form of expression poetry can be. It is a way of expressing a personal viewpoint and for the reader it is an opportunity to have access to the writer's thoughts and feelings. It is certainly a way in which they can speak to us across the centuries.

We can see this in the work of Seamus Heaney where he reflects upon what he sees and what has happened to him. His experiences have contributed to the development of his character and personality. Gillian Clarke reflects upon her own experience too and sees connections with much wider issues. 'A Difficult Birth' is addressed to her husband who she sends out to watch for the arrival of the vet. She then tells us about her involvement with the delivery of the lambs and what it meant to her – a symbol of peace in a country that, like the ewe, has been barren for such a long time. She shares this vision and this connection with us by speaking about what happened to her.

The first person style makes everything very personal. The main effect as we see in **'A Difficult Birth'** and Heaney's **'Mid-Term Break'** is that someone is speaking to us and so we become involved. The poet is sharing something with us, almost confiding in us. We can see this in John Clare's **'Sonnet'** where he is telling us exactly what appeals to him.

Other poets like William Wordsworth (**'The Affliction of Margaret'**) Thomas Hardy (**'The Man He Killed'**) and Robert Browning (**'My Last Duchess'** and **'The Laboratory'**) create new characters, someone who expresses themselves. Because they use the first person, it appears that they are speaking. We need to remember that they speak as characters, not as the poet. Robert Browning does not approve of what the Duke of Ferrara has done. By letting him speak he allows him to condemn himself. He wants the envoy to see him as a man of refinement who collects art treasures, a man who has discernment and sophistication. Of course the impression he creates is of a man who is insensitive, egotistical and brutal. This is how language works. The words you send out often mean something very different to the person who hears them.

DICTION

Key poems

Seamus Heaney	Storm on the Island
Gillian Clarke	On the Train
William Blake	The Little Boy Lost
William Blake	The Little Boy Found
Thomas Hardy	The Man He Killed
Robert Browning	My Last Duchess
Robert Browning	The Laboratory

Diction means the style and manner of speaking, the tone of voice. Poets use a way of speaking that can parallel the meaning of the thought they are trying to express or the nature of the person who is speaking. So, for example, we can see a simplicity of language in both of William Blake's poems which matches the idea of a young, innocent and inexperienced boy separated from the security of his own world. In Alfred Tennyson's **'Ulysses'** the stately verse form matches the character of the narrator.

In Seamus Heaney's **'Storm on the Island'** there is a casual conversational tone in the poem. We feel that we are being spoken to and when that happens we feel as if we are there alongside the poet as a companion. We will experience what he is describing. In **'On the Train'** Gillian Clarke successfully uses other voices in the poem. She integrates the sort of mobile phone messages with which most of us are now accustomed into the body of her poem. This serves to remind us that the accident happened to real people who lived in the real world, just as we do.

CHECK THE NET
There are lots of web sites available to help you with your revision. Try BBC Bitesize and see if you find it helpful.

If we look at **'The Laboratory'** by Robert Browning we quickly become aware of the woman's mental disturbance, not only because of what she says but also by how she says it. She shows genuine enthusiasm for what she sees, admiring the sensuous colours and the way that contrasts with the effects of the poison. She asks questions and the poet uses exclamation marks to reflect her excitement. She enjoys the idea that she will have a position of power granted to her by the poison. When we read the poem we hear her excitement, her thrill of being in control, of being able to exact her revenge. The tone of voice that is employed in **'My Last Duchess'** also helps us to make a judgement about the flawed character of the narrator. The hesitations in what the Duke of Ferrara says – 'how shall I say' (line 22) – are part of the way in which he sees himself. He is puzzled by her behaviour, implying that what he did was truly the action of a reasonable man.

The conversational tone of Thomas Hardy's **'The Man He Killed'** is particularly successful. It is so cleverly constructed, so rooted in the rhythms of speech that it almost appears not to be arranged at all. It is as if you overhear it as a conversation, that this is taken directly from real life. This adds considerably to the power of the piece.

REPETITION

> **Key poems**
>
> | | |
> |---|---|
> | Seamus Heaney | **Follower** |
> | Gillian Clarke | **On the Train** |
> | Gillian Clarke | **Baby-sitting** |
> | Charles Tichborne | **Elegy** |
> | Robert Browning | **The Laboratory** |
> | Gerard Manley Hopkins | **Inversnaid** |

The technique of repetition adds force or weight to certain ideas and phrases. It is a deliberate device, it is not accidental. A poet makes a decision to use particular words and phrases when they are writing. A whole range of words, each with a slightly different meaning, is considered and the most effective or appropriate one is chosen. So if a writer repeats something there has to be a reason for it.

Repetition of phrases

Gillian Clarke's **'On the Train'** is a good example. The repetition in lines 15 and 16 represents the phone calls made repeatedly in desperation. In her poem **'Baby-sitting'** there is repetition in the last line which expresses the impossibility of anything like maternal love for a child which is not your own. It is an emphatic end to the poem.

There is repetition of a phrase in Robert Browning's **'The Laboratory'** – 'dance at the King's' (lines 12 and 48) serves to emphasise the narrator's excitement. In Gerard Manley Hopkins' **'Inversnaid'** the repetition that dominates the last verse is a plea that places of such natural force and power should be preserved.

EXAMINER'S SECRET

Do your very best to ensure your writing is clearly formed. You don't want to lose marks because the examiner can't read your words!

Repetition of words

In Seamus Heaney's poem **'Follower'** there is an effective repetition of the word 'stumbled' in lines 13 and 23. We notice that the context of the word has changed. By the end of the poem it is his father who is stumbling, which shows how their roles have reversed, that this repeats itself not just in the poem but across generations. It connects the past and the present in an effective way.

Repetition of form

Repetition of form is part of the art of poetry that frequently involves expressing a thought in a structured way, in verses that have a pattern and a shape. For example, we see in Charles Tichborne's **'Elegy'** a repetition of form that underlines the meaning. The balance in the lines and the verses chime through the poem like the ticking of a clock. He cannot hold back time and the words and form appear to be rushing him on towards his death.

RHYME

> ### Key poems
>
> | | |
> |---|---|
> | Seamus Heaney | **At a Potato Digging** |
> | Gillian Clarke | **Cold Knap Lake** |
> | Charles Tichborne | **Elegy** |
> | William Shakespeare | **Sonnet** |
> | Gerard Manley Hopkins | **Inversnaid** |

EXAMINER'S SECRET
Learn how to spell **rhyme**. Rime means something else.

One of the effects of **rhyme** is that it creates the music in the poem; it emphasises the **rhythm** by giving the piece a regularity and a form. It is also a way of placing a stress on certain words and the ideas that they carry. It is part of the art and the technique of the poet to impose a certain shape and form and by so doing to display their skill. We can see this in the **sonnet** form that William Shakespeare uses as a frame within which to present his thoughts.

Some poets like Gillian Clarke reject the idea of rhyme, regarding it as a distraction. However, at the end of **'Cold Knap Lake'** she suddenly uses a **rhyming couplet**. It is arresting, coming as it does at the end of a poem that has no other lines that rhyme so positively. It ties the poem together, emphasising the memory at the heart of the poem. She says 'By the end of the poem the true story has almost become a legend, one I will never forget, about a child who nearly drowned in a lake, about a heroine who saved her, about a poor home and a cruel father. The fully rhyming couplet seems the right way to end a fairy story'.

DID YOU KNOW?

Gillian Clarke says 'Rhyme can be a trap. It can sound glib'.

Charles Tichborne uses rhyme deliberately in his **'Elegy'** to strike insistently, indicating the desperate on-rush of time that the poet is powerless to influence. Another good example of how rhyme can create a rhythm can be found in Gerard Manley Hopkins **'Inversnaid'** where the line endings drive the poem onward at a pace that matches the flow of the stream.

Seamus Heaney's approach to rhyme, however, is much less rigid. As we have seen in **'At a Potato Digging'** he is prepared to vary his rhyme scheme, to drop it, to re-introduce it altogether so that it adds to his purpose in writing the poem. Of course this poem then ends with the rhyme broken. It comes as a surprise and gives emphasis to the desperate and feeble offering that the workers make to keep the famine away. It is all part of our relationship with the text, expecting a rhyme and then not finding one.

Now take a break!

PART FOUR

RESOURCES

HOW TO USE QUOTATIONS

EXAMINER'S SECRET

Don't waste your time learning long quotations. Short ones are much more effective.

One of the secrets of success in writing essays is the way you use quotations. There are five basic principles:

1 Put inverted commas at the beginning and end of the quotation.

2 Write the quotation exactly as it appears in the original.

3 Do not use a quotation that repeats what you have just written.

4 Use the quotation so that it fits into your sentence.

5 Keep the quotation as short as possible.

Quotations should be used to develop the line of thought in your essays. Your comment should not duplicate what is in your quotation. For example:

> **Seamus Heaney begins 'Storm on the Island' by telling us that the people bury their homes and put slate on the roof: 'Sink walls in rock and roof them with good slate'.**

Far more effective is to write:

> **Seamus Heaney describes how the people take precautions against the storm. They 'Sink walls in rock and roof them with good slate.'**

Always lay out the lines as they appear in the text. For example:

EXAMINER'S SECRET

It is better to write about four poems in detail than to write about more but in general terms.

> We build our houses squat
> Sink walls in rock and roof them with good slate.

Or:

> 'We build our houses squat / Sink walls in rock and roof them with good slate.'

However, the most sophisticated way to use the writer's words is to embed them into your sentence:

> The people's homes are built to defend them against the storms. They are 'squat'. They are threatened by one element so they shelter in another. They 'Sink walls in rock'. The slate on their roofs is 'good'.

SITTING THE EXAMINATION

Examination papers are carefully designed to give you the opportunity to do your best. Follow these handy hints for exam success:

BEFORE YOU START

- Make sure you know the subject of the examination so that you are properly prepared and equipped.

- You need to be comfortable and free from distractions. Inform the invigilator if anything is off-putting, e.g. a shaky desk.

- Read the instructions, or rubric, on the front of the examination paper. You should know by now what you have to do but check to reassure yourself.

- Observe the time allocation – and follow it carefully. If they recommend 60 minutes for Question 1 and 30 minutes for Question 2, it is because Question 1 carries twice as many marks.

- Consider the mark allocation. You should write a longer response for 4 marks than for 2 marks.

WRITING YOUR RESPONSES

- Use the questions to structure your response, e.g. question: 'The endings of X's poems are always particularly significant. Explain their importance with reference to two poems.' The first part of your answer will describe the ending of the first poem; the second part will look at the ending of the second poem; the third

EXAMINER'S SECRET
Do plan your answer before you start. Knowing what you are going to say will make everything else much easier and it will keep your answer relevant.

EXAMINER'S SECRET
A focused answer is much more effective than a long rambling one.

part will be an explanation of the significance of the two endings.

- Write a brief draft outline of your response.

- A typical 30-minute examination essay is probably between 400 and 600 words in length.

- Keep your writing legible and easy to read, using paragraphs to show the structure of your answers.

- Spend a couple of minutes afterwards quickly checking for obvious errors.

WHEN YOU HAVE FINISHED

- Don't be downhearted – if you found the examination difficult, it is probably because you really worked at the questions. Let's face it, they are not meant to be easy!

- Don't pay too much attention to what your friends have to say about the paper. Everyone's experience is different and no two people ever give the same answers.

IMPROVE YOUR GRADE

HOW TO SELECT THE POEMS

Preserve your flexibility, keep your options open.

EXAMINER'S SECRET
Ask yourself. Why did the poet write this poem? This will help you focus on the poet's technique and purposes.

Don't forget that the poems will fit a number of themes. So stop and think which poems best fit the question you have been given. This is why a few minutes' planning is never wasted.

- Gillian Clarke's **'Catrin'** for example can fit a number of themes – relationships, love, personal involvement, conflict, memories, the past, **imagery**.

- You can do the same sort of thing with all the poems: Charles Tichborne's **'Elegy'** for example could be used in an examination of poetic technique, **rhyme**, the past, fear, worry. Seamus

Heaney's **'Death of a Naturalist'** deals with childhood, disappointment, fear, the past, imagery.

- Certainly if you look through these York Notes carefully you will see that certain titles appear more frequently than others, which might suggest they have a wider application. You cannot however rely upon such judgements entirely. Never put all your eggs in one basket labelled 'nature'!

Don't panic.

- Always remember that you **must** include one poem by Gillian Clarke and one by Seamus Heaney in any question you answer. You are also expected to include two poems from the Pre-1914 Poetry Bank. Keep this in your mind and be systematic in your planning. You know you have to write four sections on four poems so your essay is already structured for you.

- Start off by considering the nominated poem. Sketch out what you want to say in your plan and see how the main theme is treated. You could do a spider diagram with the nominated poem at the centre. Work outwards from the nominated poem. Then choose linking poems with the intention of writing about them in a systematic way. A methodical approach like this will enable you to write with confidence.

Let us imagine that you have been asked to write about the way writers deal with the theme of responsibility and the nominated poem is **'Ulysses'** by Alfred Tennyson. This poem would be our starting point and you must identify three other poems: one by Heaney, one by Clarke, and one from the Pre-1914 Poetry Bank.

❶ The title of the question would certainly point us towards **'Follower'** by Heaney and the way family relationships change and responsibility shifts. The key word in the poem, as you remember, is 'stumbled' (line 13).

❷ Now we go on to look at Gillian Clarke. There is certainly a sense of responsibility in **'Catrin'** but we can also see relevance in the poem **'Baby-sitting'** which is a task full of responsibility but one which lacks the power of the maternal instinct. So here

EXAMINER'S SECRET

Plan your time carefully to make sure you finish the paper. Time spent in planning is never wasted.

EXAMINER'S SECRET

Be ready to write about a range of poems. Don't prejudge the exam or second-guess the questions. True confidence comes from being properly prepared.

we have a choice to make, one determined largely on the basis of personal preference.

❸ From the Pre-1914 Poetry Bank. **'The Song of the Old Mother'** would certainly be relevant here, an old woman worn down by the never-ending domestic chores that she must fulfil for others.

So there we have it. We have made a selection that is appropriate and we now know how we will proceed with our answer. And this is quite a hard question too. The one in the examination will be much easier!

How to construct a response

It is obvious that the exam is going to test the things you have learnt about the poets you have studied. But it is also a test of whether or not you can actually do an examination successfully. So you need to master examination technique, keeping focused and organised and managing your time effectively. You might know all the poems inside out but if you cannot organise yourself to answer a question systematically then you are not going to score highly. So we need to think not just about **what** you are going to say but also **how** you are going to say it.

Whoever you are, you will need a plan for your essay. The biggest mistake you can make is rushing in and writing without one. A plan acts as a signpost to where you want to go and how you expect to get there. It is not a waste of time at all. It keeps you on task, focussed on the title and makes sure you fulfil the examination requirements. This is particularly important when you are attempting a complex matter like a question that asks you to select poems from different writers. No matter how brilliantly you write about Gillian Clarke, you will not score highly if you miss out Seamus Heaney altogether. So get organised.

The question

Let us assume that you are writing an answer to a question that asks about **dramatic events** and which identifies the poem **'On the Train'** by Gillian Clarke in the question itself. You will need therefore to select the other poems that you are going to deal with before you do anything else.

- This title gives you a number of choices. Let's assume that from Seamus Heaney you decide to select **'Mid-Term Break'**; from the Pre-1914 Poetry Bank you select **'My Last Duchess'** by Robert Browning and **'Patrolling Barnegat'** by Walt Whitman.

EXAMINER'S SECRET
Always look for ways in which you can cross-refer to other poems.

Introduction

- A long introduction is not necessary. But you do need to get yourself going. Once you have written a few lines you will establish a rhythm. You don't need anything elaborate. A simple statement of intent would be enough:

> **In this essay I am going to look at the way four poets present dramatic events in their poetry. I am going to write about On the Train by Gillian Clarke, Mid-Term Break by Seamus Heaney, My Last Duchess by Robert Browning and Patrolling Barnegat by Walt Whitman.**

This would be sufficient. It shows that you are in control and that you have a clear purpose and direction to your essay. However, a good candidate might add a sentence at the end such as this, which suggests that they are reflective and that they can compare and contrast texts:

> **In each of these poems we see differences in the way the poets achieve their effects and communicate a sense of drama to their reader.**

The important point is that by looking at a writer's techniques and purposes the very highest marks are achieved.

Clarke

- Start your next paragraph by looking at Gillian Clarke's poem. Remember that you are looking at how a dramatic event is presented.

Basic

An answer that only tells the story of the poem will not score highly:

Gillian Clarke is going home on the train and she tries to phone her husband on her mobile phone.

This shows that the candidate can remember some of the elements in the first verse but it is not the sort of start that inspires confidence.

Better

A better start would be:

As she travels home on the train the day after the Paddington rail crash, Gillian Clarke is worried and wants reassurance that everything is all right at home.

Here we have a C/D-grade candidate realising that the dramatic event that needs to be referred to in the essay took place on the previous day. The poet therefore *reflects* on the events of the disaster:

Since she is also travelling on a train she can put herself into the situation of the victims.

Best

An A/B-grade candidate will show their quality in a more detailed response that looks at how the train journey is placed in a context and how the language the poet uses creates the mood:

As Gillian Clarke travels home on the train she is full of apprehension. The fields are flooded, her Walkman is described as a 'black box' (line 3) which reminds us of a flight recorder and her tea 'trembles' (line 4) in its cup. It is the day after the Paddington rail crash and she needs to hear a voice of reassurance from home. The previous day unsuspecting passengers were killed as they got on with their ordinary everyday lives.

What we can see is close textual reference that indicates the significance of the writer's word choice. The paragraph here uses short effective quotations that are embedded in the body of the text. Such quotations as these are easy to learn too. These are the qualities that distinguish the best candidates.

Heaney

- When you have finished **'On the Train'** move on to your next poem in a new paragraph. It is easier to maintain the order of the poems that you established in your introduction. At least in this way you will not get lost.

Basic

A candidate operating at a basic level will continue to rely upon remembering the story of the death of the poet's brother.

Better

Better candidates will again *reflect* on what happens:

> **Seamus Heaney knows that something unusual has happened because his school does not seem to know what to do with him. They make him wait to be collected in the sick bay, which is ironic because his brother is in hospital.**

Best

The best candidates focus upon how the writer achieves his effects:

> **Seamus Heaney is made to wait in the college sick bay whilst his brother is dead in the hospital. The second line of the poem is dominated by the sound of the letter 'l' which emphasises the sound of the bells. To the school boys these bells mark the change of lessons but they also seem to toll to mark Heaney's loss.**

You can see that to access the higher marks you must try to integrate comments on the effects of the language into your writing. It is also clear that detailed writing is always going to score more highly than writing that uses general comments. Look at these two samples and assess which one will get the higher mark.

> 1. **When he arrives home Seamus Heaney is greeted by his father on the porch. He is distressed. The young boy is embarrassed by all the attention he receives.**

EXAMINER'S SECRET

Start each of your answers on a new page in your examination answer book. If you leave a little space at the end of each answer you can always add additional comments later.

2. When he arrives home Seamus Heaney finds himself in an unusual situation for his father who 'had always taken funerals in his stride' is clearly distressed and greets him at the porch. The local community seems to have gathered together to express solidarity. The poet says nothing at all. He seems numb, detached.

It should be clear that the second sample is more successful because it contains more detail.

Pre-1914 poem 1

You should continue with your systematic approach, working through the poems you have chosen in the order you identified. Your next poem is **'My Last Duchess'** by Robert Browning. Once again the use of well-supported detailed comments will achieve the higher marks. Here the dramatic event you are referring to is the conversation between the Duke and the envoy. You cannot write about the murder of the Duchess because we do not see it in the poem. So like the poem itself you must concentrate on the conversation. The drawing back of the curtain to reveal the painting is certainly a dramatic moment itself and you could make this the part of the poem you will explore.

This is an important point. You do not always need to write about a whole poem. You can choose a significant moment and write about that moment in detail. This is much better than trying to summarise the whole of a long and complex poem within the context of an examination essay.

Pre-1914 poem 2

You have now reached your last poem, **'Patrolling Barnegat'** by Walt Whitman, which explores the drama of a storm at sea. As we have said before, the comments that examine the effect of his language will be the most successful. You can say that the poem uses the same sounds throughout but what you need to say is that the repetition of the sounds represents the relentless pounding of the waves. That is the point. It is not enough to say what the effects **are**. You must say what the effects **do** and **how** they contribute to the meaning or the mood of the poem. It is this awareness of the writer

as someone who does things quite deliberately for the effect that
they have, that marks out the best candidates and gets them the
highest marks.

**EXAMINER'S
SECRET**
Don't write 'it says'.
Write instead 'the
poet says'.

Conclusion

This is not the place to introduce new information. You should
bring your essay round full circle. Say that you have examined these
dramatic poems and that the poets' skills have involved you in the
events they have described. This is the place to express your
preferences. Remember to remain positive and to express your
interest in what you have read.

Writing a conclusion is an important skill, showing you can start,
develop an idea and then bring it all to a coherent ending, all in a
limited amount of time.

SAMPLE ESSAY PLAN

To help with your revision and your planning, here is a sample
question and answer. Remember, this does not represent the only
answer to this question. This is merely one suggestion. Do not
forget either that this is only an outline.

> Compare the ways that poets write about love in 4 or more of
> the poems you have studied.
> You should write about William Shakespeare's 'Sonnet 130'
> and compare it with at least one poem by Gillian Clarke, one
> by Seamus Heaney and with one other poem from the Pre-
> 1914 Poetry Bank.

INTRODUCTION
Your introduction could begin with a basic statement:

> Love has been one of the basic themes in artistic expression
> throughout history. We can see today how the worlds of
> music and film are dominated by the idea of love.

This is a high-level response and shows that you are capable of reflecting upon an issue and shows that you are approaching the task with confidence.

EXAMINER'S SECRET

Identifying the four poems in your introduction shows that your essay is deliberate and planned. Put the poem nominated by the examiners first.

Go on to express your intent. You are going to look at four poets who explore different aspects of love. Then say which poems you are going to look at:

- William Shakespeare's **'Sonnet 130'**
- Gillian Clarke's **'Catrin'**
- Seamus Heaney's **'Follower'**
- Robert Browning's **'The Laboratory'**

There are two ways of proceeding now. You can either deal with each poem in turn or you can move between them, dealing with the poems in parallel. A lot depends upon your personal preference and upon the question. It is certainly easy to maintain control and to ensure coverage of the requirements if you treat each poem separately.

Part 1

Write about William Shakespeare's **'Sonnet 130'**, remembering that the focus of the question must be upon love. He rejects conventional behaviour. He does not use exaggeration or elaborate comparisons.

You should then show how William Shakespeare achieves this. It is by looking at the words and the structure that you will achieve high marks. A quotation always helps and a good one here would be '**My mistress when she walks treads on the ground**' (line 1), which shows that he regards her as a real person.

Part 2

Move on now to examine the next poem. Say that you have moved from romantic love to consider the love that exists between the generations in the next two poems. Notice that you are confirming a further link between the poems you have chosen, **'Catrin'** and **'Follower'**.

EXAMINER'S SECRET

Make sure that you know who wrote which poem! Get their names right!

Gillian Clarke's poem explores the love between a mother and her daughter. You should then go on to examine the central image in the poem and explain its significance. This is of course the image of the rope. They were once one person who became two but the emotional connection remains. A good quotation to introduce would be 'Red rope of love' (line 8).

PART 3

Now move on to look at Seamus Heaney's **'Follower'**. Say that both poems bring together the past and the present. Indicate that one of the elements in a relationship between parents and their children is responsibility. Gillian Clarke reveals this in her relationship with her daughter because of her concern for her safety. In Seamus Heaney's poem we see how their roles are eventually reversed over time. Notice how these comments maintain the links between these two poems and indicate that the writer has engaged fully with the texts.

In **'Follower'** we see the respect and love he has for his father. He expresses his admiration for his skill. A useful quotation to include would be 'His shoulders globed' (line 2) because this indicates how he filled Seamus Heaney's world, and it puts the emphasis not upon story but upon **imagery** and technique.

Finish this section by showing how their roles now have been reversed. Refer to the use of the words 'stumbled' (line 13) and 'stumbling' (line 23).

PART 4

Move on to the last poem, indicating that the writer here explores a completely different aspect of love, love gone wrong. Robert Browning's **'The Laboratory'** is a **dramatic monologue** in which a character reveals herself through what she says.

We only ever see the woman's side of the story so we cannot form a judgement about the truth of what happened. Her lover has left her for someone else and she is so distressed she wants revenge by poisoning her rival.

Write about how she enjoys the power that the poison will bring her. Contrast this love with the love in the other poems you have looked at. Is this love about possession and power?

EXAMINER'S SECRET

The danger in using one of Robert Browning's poems is that you could find yourself drawn into explaining the story. What you must do to avoid this is to write about **how** we find out about the character and by referring back to the original question.

EXAMINER'S SECRET

This sort of reflective comment which draws the texts together shows that you can see connections, evaluate and draw conclusions.

EXAMINER'S SECRET

Don't waste time with correction fluid. Just put a neat line through anything you want to cancel and then get back to your writing.

EXAMINER'S SECRET

If you can, give yourself a couple of minutes to read it through to check for any glaring errors. After all if you can't be bothered to read it why should an examiner?

CONCLUSION

Keep it brief. Try not to repeat what you said in the introduction. Say that you have looked at family love, romantic love and love that has turned to obsession. These poems span the ages and show it is a universal theme. Indicate your own preferences and reactions. What were your feelings as you read them?

FURTHER QUESTIONS

These suggested examination questions are presented in the sort of format that is used in the examinations and use the broad themes that are discussed in these York Notes. They are not intended to be either complete or exclusive and of course other words could be used to identify a topic that is very close to these here. So you could replace 'the natural world' or 'animals' in the question about 'nature' and have a very similar question. You could also substitute 'suffering' or 'death' for 'sad poems'. So keep an open mind.

❶ Look at the ways in which the poets think about the **past**.

You should write about **'Cold Knap Lake'** by Gillian Clarke, and compare it with at least **one** poem by Seamus Heaney and **two** poems from the Pre-1914 Poetry Bank.

❷ Compare the ways that poets present **a feeling of disappointment** in **four or more** of the poems you have studied.

You should write about Seamus Heaney's **'Blackberry-Picking'** and compare it with least **one** poem by Gillian Clarke and **two** poems from the Pre-1914 Poetry Bank.

❸ There are a number of occasions in these poems when the poet shows **admiration** for another person.

You should write about Seamus Heaney's **'Digging'** and compare it with least **one** poem by Gillian Clarke and **two** poems from the Pre-1914 Poetry Bank.

❹ Examine the ways in which poets in this selection write about **family relationships**.

You should write about **'Catrin'** by Gillian Clarke and compare it with at least **one** poem by Seamus Heaney and **two** poems from the Pre-1914 Poetry Bank.

5 There is a range of different emotions presented in these poems, ranging from sorrow to happiness. Compare the ways that the poets present **their feelings** in **four or more** of the poems you have studied.

You should write about Seamus Heaney's **'Mid-Term Break'** and compare it with at least **one** poem by Gillian Clarke and **two** poems from the Pre-1914 Poetry Bank.

6 In Alfred Tennyson's poem **'Ulysses'** the King of Ithaca wants to leave his responsibilities behind. Look at the way the poets here write about **responsibility**.

You should write about **'Ulysses'** by Alfred Tennyson and compare it with at least **one** poem by Gillian Clarke, **one** by Seamus Heaney and with **one** other poem from the Pre-1914 Poetry Bank.

7 You might think that **'Elegy'** by Charles Tichborne is a very sad poem.

Compare this with at least **three** others you have studied which might be seen as **sad poems**. Write about at least **one** poem by Gillian Clarke, **one** by Seamus Heaney and with **one** other poem from the Pre-1914 Poetry Bank.

8 Compare the ways that poets use **memorable imagery** in **four or more** of the poems you have studied.

You should write about Seamus Heaney's **'At a Potato Picking'** and compare it with least **one** poem by Gillian Clarke and **two** poems from the Pre-1914 Poetry Bank.

9 Compare the ways in which the poets in this selection write about **nature**. You should write about **'The Field-Mouse'** by Gillian Clarke and compare it with at least **one** poem by Seamus Heaney and **two** poems from the Pre-1914 Poetry Bank.

10 Compare the ways that poets write about **children** in **four or more** of the poems you have studied.

You should write about Seamus Heaney's **'Death of a Naturalist'** and compare it with least **one** poem by Gillian Clarke and **two** poems from the Pre-1914 Poetry Bank.

EXAMINER'S SECRET

If you do not have enough time for a conclusion then don't worry. Leave it out and move on to the next question. If you do have time a conclusion rounds things off nicely.

EXAMINER'S SECRET

Don't be afraid to express an opinion but be prepared to support it.

EXAMINER'S SECRET

Keep the words of the question in front of you to help you remain relevant in your answer.

LITERARY TERMS

allegory a story or situation written in such a way as to have two coherent meanings

alliteration a sequence of repeated sounds in a stretch of language

ambiguity the capacity of words and sentences to have double meanings

anapaest a trisyllabic metrical foot, consisting of two unstressed syllables followed by a stressed syllable – ti-ti-tum

antithetic parallelisms opposing or contrasting ideas in next-door sentences or clauses

assonance the correspondence, or near correspondence, in two words of the stressed vowel, e.g. c<u>a</u>n and f<u>a</u>t, ch<u>i</u>ld and s<u>i</u>lence

atmosphere a mood or feeling that dominates a poem

blank verse unrhymed **iambic pentameter** – a line of five lines

blazon a description of a woman's beauty in list form

cadenced the rhythm of prose or verse caused by the various stresses placed on syllables and words

caesura a pause within a line of verse

cliché a boring phrase or word, made tedious by frequent repetition

colloquialism expressions and grammar associated with ordinary, everyday speech

conceit a special sort of **figurative** device, usually a simile

connotation the secondary meanings of a word, what it suggests or implies

couplet a pair of rhymed lines of any **metre**

decorum use of the proper and fitting style for every literary kind

diction the choice of words in a work of literature

dramatic monologue a poem in which a specific person, not the poet, is speaking

elegy a poem lamenting the death of a particular person

ellipsis in grammar the omission of words thought to be essential in the complete form of the sentence

end-stopped verse a line of verse in which the end of the line coincides with an essential pause

enjambment a line of poetry that is not **end-stopped**, in which the sentence continues into the next line

epic a long narrative poem about the exploits of super-human heroes or gods

epigraphs quotation or fragment placed at the beginning of poems, chapters or novels as a clue to their meaning

epitaph an inscription on a tomb, or piece of writing suitable for that purpose

euphemism word or phrase that is less blunt or terrifying, e.g. 'pass away' = die

euphony language that sounds pleasant and musical.

figurative language any form of expression or grammar that departs from the plainest expression of meaning

half-rhyme an imperfect rhyme

heroic couplet lines of **iambic pentameters** rhymed in pairs

iamb a weak stress followed by a strong stress, ti-tum

iambic pentameter a line of five **iambic** feet

image a picture which words create in the mind of a reader

imagery any figurative language (metaphors and similes)

irony saying one thing while you mean another

Masculine rhyme a monosyllabic rhyme on the final stressed syllable of two lines of verse

metaphor a metaphor is when two different things are fused together; one thing described as another thing

metre the pattern of stressed and unstressed syllables in a line of verse

monologue single person speaking with or without an audience is uttering a monologue

motif dominant/recurring idea or theme in literary or musical composition

myth story usually concerning super-humans or gods

onomatopoeia words which sound like the noise which they describe

oxymoron a figure of speech in which contrasting terms are brought together

pun a play on words

quatrain a verse or group of four lines

realism the representation of 'ordinary' life

refrain recurring phrase or line at end of stanza

rhyme the deliberate matching of sounds that creates an audible attern

rhyming couplet two-line rhyme

rhythm in poetry the chief element of rhythm is the variation in levels of stress accorded to the syllables

simile a figure of speech in which one thing is said to be like another

sonnet a fourteen line poem written to one of a number of established patterns

subtext a word for the situation that lies behind the behaviour of the characters in a play

symbol something which represents something else

syntax the arrangement of words in their appropriate forms and proper order

tone the sense of a particular mood or manner in which a passage should be read

tragic in literature, it is 'tragic' when an individual experiences a downfall as a result of both their strengths and their weaknesses

CHECKPOINT HINTS/ANSWERS

CHECKPOINT 1 The earth offers shelter to the people facing the power of the storm.

CHECKPOINT 2 The poem is all one sentence, perhaps suggesting the constant movement of the river.

CHECKPOINT 3 As a rat.

CHECKPOINT 4 Taste.

CHECKPOINT 5 Green, blue, yellow, brown.

CHECKPOINT 6 A spade.

CHECKPOINT 7 The rhyme is found in the last two lines and it makes us work out his brother's age.

CHECKPOINT 8 Snowdrops which are white and stress the child's pallor against which the bright red of the poppy reference contrasts sharply.

CHECKPOINT 9 He is copying the actions of an expert ploughman as described in lines 10 to 12.

CHECKPOINT 10 There is the comparison of the turf to the sea at the end of the line and so the men gathering the potatoes are like fishermen.

CHECKPOINT 11 The poem explores the relationship between a mother and daughter. Therefore there is no need to write about Catrin's father.

CHECKPOINT 12 Touch. The baby will not want the baby-sitter to touch her.

CHECKPOINT 13 They have been picking blackberries.

CHECKPOINT 14 The reference to amniotic fluid.

CHECKPOINT 15 A blade and a gun.

CHECKPOINT 16 They are both negative references, suggesting bad news.

CHECKPOINT 17 The death of her close friend.

CHECKPOINT 18 A sense of the comfort and security of home.

CHECKPOINT 19 They alternate between four and six lines until we reach the final couplet.

CHECKPOINT 20 He says that his son was his best piece of poetry.

CHECKPOINT 21 The metre is heavily stressed and can be clearly heard when the poem is read aloud. It is a combination of iambs ('I rise') and anapests ('In the dawn').

CHECKPOINT 22 The poem contains examples of what, in its time, would have been considered ordinary speech ('I dread the rustling of the grass' line 65; 'I question things' line 68). Wordsworth rejected conventional poetic language and preferred to use 'a selection of language really used by men' ('Preface to Lyrical Ballads').

CHECKPOINT 23 The fact that it was written just before the young Tichborne was horribly executed must make it especially moving to the reader.

CHECKPOINT 24 Tichborne does use a repeated metaphorical device throughout the poem, but the repetition could be said to increase the sense of a doomed young man 'adding up' what his life means.

CHECKPOINT 25 With a very ironic tone of voice!

CHECKPOINT 26 Whitman combines both the effects of alliteration and onomatopoeia in phrases like 'slush and sand' (line 6) and 'swirl and spray' (line 8) to communicate the physical effects of the storm and the shore.

CHECKPOINT 27 They would probably respond to the honesty of a poem that stresses their appeal as a real person.

CHECKPOINT 28 She was innocent and lively, unaware of the affect she was having on her husband.

CHECKPOINT 29 In order to stress his reasonable nature. After all he is negotiating a new marriage.

CHECKPOINT 30 It now gives him complete control over her. Also he regards his art collection as his own property to be made and to be viewed on his own terms. See the last word of the poem.

CHECKPOINT 31 It shows how excited the woman is at the prospect of revenge.

CHECKPOINT 32 She wants to believe that her lover was trapped by this other woman, that he did not desert her of his own choice.

CHECKPOINT 33 It means death.

CHECKPOINT 34 He has a very low opinion of them. He thinks he is far more sophisticated than they are.

CHECKPOINT 35 The fact that he knew lots of long words that sounded impressive.

CHECKPOINT 36 Claws. They are suggested by the hard 'c' sounds.

CHECKPOINT 37 Possibly in the image of the horse in the first line.

CHECKPOINT 38 The word that is repeated at the beginning of some of the lines is 'I'.

SEAMUS HEANEY

1 Storm on the Island

2 Blackberry-Picking

3 Death of a Naturalist

4 Follower

5 At a Potato Digging

6 The Bann river

7 In the college sick bay

8 On the farm

9 The flax-dam

10 Storm on the Island

11 Death of a Naturalist

12 At a Potato Digging

GILLIAN CLARKE

1 Catrin

2 Baby-sitting

3 A Difficult Birth

4 The Field-Mouse

5 October

6 On the Train

7 Cold Knap Lake

8 Mali

9 A Difficult Birth

10 Catrin

11 Cold Knap Lake

12 The Field-Mouse

PRE-1914 POETRY BANK

1 The song of the Old Mother (W. B. Yeats)

2 The Affliction of Margaret (William Wordsworth)

3 Elegy (Charles Tichborne)

4 Sonnet (William Shakespeare)

5 The Village Schoolmaster (Oliver Goldsmith)

6 Inversnaid (Gerard Manley Hopkins)

7 Sonnet (John Clare)

8 The Man He Killed (Thomas Hardy)

9 Patrolling Barnegat (Walt Whitman)

10 The Little Boy Lost (William Blake)

11 Tichborne's Elegy (Charles Tichborne)

12 The Little Boy Found (William Blake)

13 The Song of the Old Mother (W. B. Yeats)

14 On my first Sonne (Ben Jonson)

15 Sonnet 130 (William Shakespeare)

16 The Laboratory (Robert Browning)

17 My Last Duchess (Robert Browning)

18 The Village Schoolmaster (Oliver Goldsmith)

19 Ulysses (Alfred Tennyson)

20 Sonnet (John Clare)

21 Inversnaid (Gerard Manley Hopkins)

22 The Eagle (Alfred Tennyson)

Maya Angelou
*I Know Why the Caged Bird
Sings*

Jane Austen
Pride and Prejudice

Alan Ayckbourn
Absent Friends

Elizabeth Barrett Browning
Selected Poems

Robert Bolt
A Man for All Seasons

Harold Brighouse
Hobson's Choice

Charlotte Brontë
Jane Eyre

Emily Brontë
Wuthering Heights

Shelagh Delaney
A Taste of Honey

Charles Dickens
*David Copperfield
Great Expectations
Hard Times
Oliver Twist*

Roddy Doyle
Paddy Clarke Ha Ha Ha

George Eliot
*Silas Marner
The Mill on the Floss*

Anne Frank
The Diary of a Young Girl

William Golding
Lord of the Flies

Oliver Goldsmith
She Stoops to Conquer

Willis Hall
*The Long and the Short and the
Tall*

Thomas Hardy
Far from the Madding Crowd

*The Mayor of Casterbridge
Tess of the d'Urbervilles
The Withered Arm and other
Wessex Tales*

L.P. Hartley
The Go-Between

Seamus Heaney
Selected Poems

Susan Hill
I'm the King of the Castle

Barry Hines
A Kestrel for a Knave

Louise Lawrence
Children of the Dust

Harper Lee
To Kill a Mockingbird

Laurie Lee
Cider with Rosie

Arthur Miller
*The Crucible
A View from the Bridge*

Robert O'Brien
Z for Zachariah

Frank O'Connor
*My Oedipus Complex and
Other Stories*

George Orwell
Animal Farm

J.B. Priestley
*An Inspector Calls
When We Are Married*

Willy Russell
*Educating Rita
Our Day Out*

J.D. Salinger
The Catcher in the Rye

William Shakespeare
*Henry IV Part I
Henry V
Julius Caesar*

*Macbeth
The Merchant of Venice
A Midsummer Night's Dream
Much Ado About Nothing
Romeo and Juliet
The Tempest
Twelfth Night*

George Bernard Shaw
Pygmalion

Mary Shelley
Frankenstein

R.C. Sherriff
Journey's End

Rukshana Smith
Salt on the snow

John Steinbeck
Of Mice and Men

Robert Louis Stevenson
Dr Jekyll and Mr Hyde

Jonathan Swift
Gulliver's Travels

Robert Swindells
Daz 4 Zoe

Mildred D. Taylor
Roll of Thunder, Hear My Cry

Mark Twain
Huckleberry Finn

James Watson
Talking in Whispers

Edith Wharton
Ethan Frome

William Wordsworth
Selected Poems

A Choice of Poets

*Mystery Stories of the Nineteenth
Century including The Signalman*

*Nineteenth Century Short
Stories*

Poetry of the First World War

*Six Women Poets*aret Atwood

Margaret Atwood
Cat's Eye
The Handmaid's Tale

Jane Austen
Emma
Mansfield Park
Persuasion
Pride and Prejudice
Sense and Sensibility

Alan Bennett
Talking Heads

William Blake
Songs of Innocence and of
Experience

Charlotte Brontë
Jane Eyre
Villette

Emily Brontë
Wuthering Heights

Angela Carter
Nights at the Circus

Geoffrey Chaucer
The Franklin's Prologue and Tale
The Miller's Prologue and Tale
The Prologue to the Canterbury
Tales
The Wife of Bath's Prologue and
Tale

Samuel Coleridge
Selected Poems

Joseph Conrad
Heart of Darkness

Daniel Defoe
Moll Flanders

Charles Dickens
Bleak House
Great Expectations
Hard Times

Emily Dickinson
Selected Poems

John Donne
Selected Poems

Carol Ann Duffy
Selected Poems

George Eliot
Middlemarch
The Mill on the Floss

T.S. Eliot
Selected Poems
The Waste Land

F. Scott Fitzgerald
The Great Gatsby

E.M. Forster
A Passage to India

Brian Friel
Translations

Thomas Hardy
Jude the Obscure
The Mayor of Casterbridge
The Return of the Native
Selected Poems
Tess of the d'Urbervilles

Seamus Heaney
Selected Poems from 'Opened
Ground'

Nathaniel Hawthorne
The Scarlet Letter

Homer
The Iliad
The Odyssey

Aldous Huxley
Brave New World

Kazuo Ishiguro
The Remains of the Day

Ben Jonson
The Alchemist

James Joyce
Dubliners

John Keats
Selected Poems

Christopher Marlowe
Doctor Faustus
Edward II

Arthur Miller
Death of a Salesman

John Milton
Paradise Lost Books I & II

Toni Morrison
Beloved

George Orwell
Nineteen Eighty-Four

Sylvia Plath
Selected Poems

Alexander Pope
Rape of the Lock & Selected
Poems

William Shakespeare
Antony and Cleopatra
As You Like It
Hamlet
Henry IV Part I
King Lear
Macbeth
Measure for Measure
The Merchant of Venice
A Midsummer Night's Dream
Much Ado About Nothing
Othello
Richard II
Richard III
Romeo and Juliet
The Taming of the Shrew
The Tempest
Twelfth Night
The Winter's Tale

George Bernard Shaw
Saint Joan

Mary Shelley
Frankenstein

Jonathan Swift
Gulliver's Travels and A Modest
Proposal

Alfred Tennyson
Selected Poems

Virgil
The Aeneid

Alice Walker
The Color Purple

Oscar Wilde
The Importance of Being Earnest

Tennessee Williams
A Streetcar Named Desire

Jeanette Winterson
Oranges Are Not the Only Fruit

John Webster
The Duchess of Malfi

Virginia Woolf
To the Lighthouse

W.B. Yeats
Selected Poems

Metaphysical Poets